THE Eco-conscious
TRAVEL GUIDE

HarperCollins*Publishers*
1 London Bridge Street
London SE1 9GF

www.harpercollins.co.uk

HarperCollins*Publishers*
1st Floor, Watermarque Building, Ringsend Road
Dublin 4, Ireland

First published by HarperCollins*Publishers* 2022

10 9 8 7 6 5 4 3 2 1

A catalogue record of this book is available from the British Library.

HB ISBN 978-0-00-842425-1

Printed and bound by GPS Group, Slovenia

MIX
Paper from
responsible sources
FSC™ C007454

This book is produced from independently certified FSC™ paper
to ensure responsible forest management.

For more information visit: www.harpercollins.co.uk/green

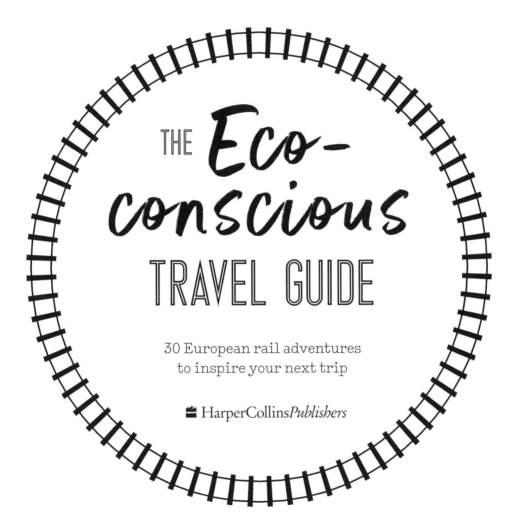

THE Eco-conscious TRAVEL GUIDE

30 European rail adventures
to inspire your next trip

HarperCollins*Publishers*

Contents

Introduction

Holidays, adventures and travel make us who we are, keep us sane and broaden our horizons. However, we are waking up to the realisation that a fast-paced lifestyle isn't necessarily better for our minds, or for the planet. Gone are the days when frantically ticking off the overpopulated hotspots of the world would be considered a relaxing, restorative break. Instead mindful, sustainable travel is what we now crave. Travelling by train gives us the chance to awaken our senses to a new place, the time to get a feel for its ebb and flow and the space to quieten the bustle of our busy minds. It also restores the balance between tourist and local, environment and economy, conservation and community.

Separated into thirty themed routes, the information in these pages provides a guiding light to help you plan your next adventure. From finding a different side to European capitals to discovering more unusual destinations (such as a Norwegian mountain only accessible by train), and whether you have a long weekend or a few weeks to spare, this book will help you to enjoy and explore Europe in a way that is good for the planet – and all while keeping you well away from stressful airports!

Most routes are circular, so you can choose to start and end your adventure anywhere you like along the way. Some explore one country in depth, others straddle several borders and cultures. There are tips scattered throughout to help you extend your trip should you want to, or use the index at the back to make up your own route.

Most of the stops on each route are via train, but there are a couple of bus journeys thrown in to mix it up a little. All journey times are correct at the time of writing, but we recommend double-checking when plotting your adventure, especially if travelling at weekends or late at night.

As well as cutting down on your carbon emissions (hurrah!), you'll also be helping to spread the tourism burden. Overtourism (see p.10) is killing some destinations (most major European cities, for example), so by choosing to visit off-season and exploring lesser-known alternatives, you will not only help to boost local economies where they need it most, but also to thin out the crowds of tourists dragging their wheeled suitcases across the capital cities.

Each destination's themed mini-guide picks up things to do and see, with a fantastic mix of cultural experiences, as well as outdoor activities – including walks, parks and picnic spots – so that you can enjoy it like a local and stay away from the queues outside the 'main attractions'. Rediscover the joy of travel, and steer clear of the clichéd online bucket lists. Soak up the sounds, sights and smells of each place and then, best of all, get back on the train and let it all seep into your soul.

Essential Eco-conscious Travel Tips

Unless you walk everywhere, camp under the stars and forage for your food, no matter how you travel, it will always have an impact on the planet. But you can reduce that impact drastically by becoming a much more sustainable traveller.

ECO-HOTELS

You might be hostelling it, renting apartments or living it up in a series of five-star hotels, but whatever your accommodation plans, there will be eco-friendly options. There is a lot of greenwashing among hotels but a truly 'eco-friendly' hotel needs to do more than offer to wash your towels less often and eradicate plastic water bottles. It needs to demonstrate what it is doing to reduce its carbon emissions and waste, tell you how it's getting its electricity, how it's helping the local community and how it employs its staff. There are some fabulously pioneering eco-hotels in Europe, and more and more booking platforms dedicated to them.

CONSERVATION

Part of being a sustainable traveller is making sure you're giving back to the place you're visiting in one form or another. This doesn't just mean contributing to the local economy or donating to charity, but also weaving experiences into your trip which directly support local conservation. From visiting nature reserves to booking wildlife or other tours that employ local guides, your holiday can leave a positive impact in so many ways. As always, the key is research and if you're not sure, ask questions! Also, share what you're doing to help to start the conversations that will lead to a greener planet.

OVER- AND UNDERTOURISM

Throughout this book we talk about overtourism, which is the flooding of tourists into particular destinations, so that they outnumber local residents and unfavourably impact the local economy and community. Venice, Bruges, Amsterdam and Barcelona are all overtourism hotspots, and while they are not avoided completely in this book, you will be guided away from the same old must-do listicles that add to the problem. It also helps to go to these places off-season to spread the love all year round and to make sure the money you spend is going into the local economy (for example, by not just staying in global chain hotels and shopping at international brands).

Undertourism is the opposite of overtourism. It relates to destinations that aren't well known to tourists – secondary and tertiary cities that have plenty to offer travellers and, arguably, give you a much more authentic local experience. There are lots of these stops in this book, as this is my favourite way to travel. There are no queues for museums or attractions and I like to spend time lingering in cafés and bars imagining what life is like here.

TRAVELLING
PLASTIC FREE

Even the most eco-aware of us tend to leave our plastic-free credentials at home when we go on holiday. But with a bit of simple planning there's no need to add to another country's plastic problem. Here are the go-to packing essentials to make sure you don't have to reach for single-use products when you're away.

BAGS Pack a variety of lightweight tote bags, so you don't get caught out at any shops or markets and find yourself needing a single-use carrier bag for all your lovely trinkets.

REUSABLE BOTTLE Not only is this essential because it stops you picking up (and paying for) single-use plastic bottles of water, it will come into its own if you're spending time on the beach or going for a picnic. The stainless-steel vacuum ones keep your cold drinks cold for twenty-four hours and hot drinks hot (perfect for a long train journey) for twelve hours.

REUSABLE CUP Similarly, think of how many to-go morning coffees you might get through on your adventure across Europe. You can avoid all that single-use-cup nonsense with a reusable one. There are even collapsible styles if space is an issue.

REUSABLE CUTLERY SET There are plenty of these out there – made from metal or bamboo, they come in a convenient roll, often with a reusable straw as well. From grabbing a quick lunch at a train station to heading out on a picnic, once you add this to your bag, it will become a daily essential.

PLASTIC-FREE HAIR/SKINCARE Space in the suitcase is always an issue, right? But you can skip the need for using plastic hotel miniatures or lugging your own full-size toiletries across Europe by swapping to shampoo, shaving and shower bars. There are so many brands offering these now, especially vegan-friendly or chemical-free ones. Invest in metal tins to store them in, and you're good to go, whether you're camping or cosying up in a posh hotel. Similarly, there are plastic-free deodorants and sun-cream options available, too.

EAT, DRINK & BE MERRY

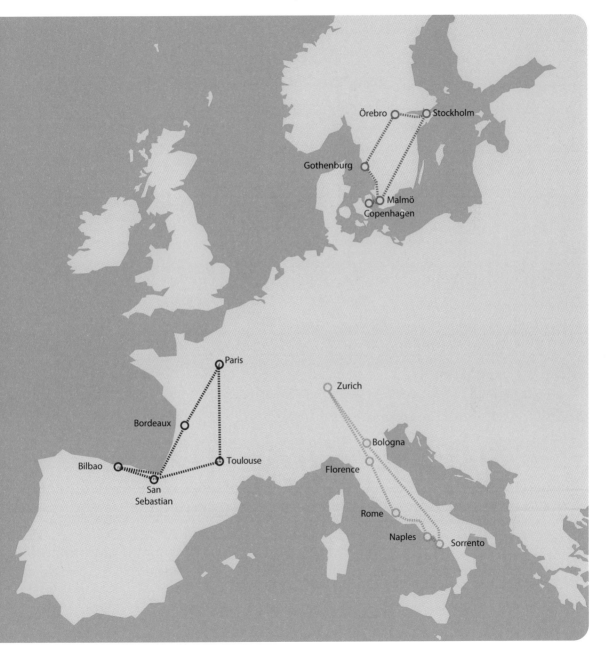

Wine-fuelled Wanders

The train makes it easy to tick off the big culinary tickets of France and the Basque country, all washed down with delicious local wine. From feasting on belly-warming dinners to nibbling on endlessly inventive *pintxos* (hot and cold bar snacks), this trip is a must for curious and classic foodies.

PARIS

Paris itself needs no introduction, but the last few years have seen a resurgence of the city's humble French bistro (often reimagined in Scandi-minimal tones) and some incredible cocktail and bio wine bars. From Gare du Nord, head south-east and wander the cobbled streets of Belleville, La Pigelle and Le Marais for *vin méthode nature* (natural wine), seasonal sharing plates and plenty of café-culture-meets-craft-brew vibes. Frenchie was one of the catalysts for this new bistro appreciation, but don't miss old-school hidden gems like Juveniles, for unpretentious but brilliant *plats du jour*, alongside its famous wine list. Make like a real Parisian and shake off the night before with locally roasted coffee from Ten Belles and a finger-licking patisserie from one of the gorgeous boulangeries in Canal Saint-Martin.

TOULOUSE

5 hrs 30 mins

Often overlooked for the Dordogne to the north or the coast to the south, Toulouse is a secondary city worth a stop. Tick off La Ville Rose's (named after all the red brick) major attractions with a two-hour walking tour, and work up an appetite for its famous *cassoulet* (a hearty sausage and bean stew). Vegans might struggle here because everything is drenched in butter, cream, cheese and chocolate, but if you're ok with that, you're going to love this compact city. Kick off the day with warm *chocolatines* (pains au chocolat, to you and me), then pick up cheese, *saucisson*, pork rillettes and head to the Jardin Japonais for a pretty picnic. Come the evening, it's all about the duck confit (foie gras is still big business here, too).

SAN SEBASTIAN

5 hrs 58 mins

There's no better way to arrive in San Sebastian than by train, having picked up a good bottle of wine in Toulouse. This tiny beach town on the Basque coast has Michelin stars by the bucketload, but some of its best food can be sampled by bar hopping and trying the *pintxos*. Don't be put off by unassuming façades – hit Calle Peña y Goñi in Gros and the tiny streets of the Old Town for super-fresh seasonal veg, salted cod, cured sardines on toast and Spanish ham and cheese-based delights.

TIP

Don't miss kicking off every evening with la hora del vermut (Vermouth hour). Seriously, it's a thing.

BILBAO

1 hr 38 mins Bilbao is known for its modern art and architecture, but the Basque capital doesn't disappoint in the food stakes either. Head for Casco Viejo and Plaza Nueva in Bilbao la Vieja for hip bars, yet more *pintxos* (baby squid in ink are a city speciality) and restaurants for every budget. Dine in family institutions from the Twenties, retro Fifties' diners or *txakoli*, which serve rustic food and lashings of local white wine. Don't miss the city's unique underwater wine cellar, where you can taste on land or at sea and the huge 1920s Art Deco covered food market, Mercado de la Ribera, once Europe's largest.

BORDEAUX

5 hrs 15 mins

The wine capital of France has had a makeover. The Cité du Vin runs workshops and talks, while the tourist board has created an Urban Wine Trail, where you can discover the huge array of producers across the city's best wine bars. If you have time, spend a couple of days on vineyard tours – there are thousands of châteaux to pick from. But it's not all about the wine here. Borrow a bike (Bordeaux is very bike friendly), grab some freshly prepared oysters at the Marché des Quais, take in the famous Water Mirror and the neo-classical Place de la Bourse and finish off with the city's iconic *canelé* (a rich, dark rum cake). *Journey time back to Paris:* 2 hrs 44 mins

SORRENTO · NAPELS · ROME · FLORENCE · ZURICH · BOLOGNA

Les Monts Ysingeais

Chocolate, Cheese & Carb Delights

Better pack the leisurewear for this circular route. It's a full-on cheese, carbs and chocolate fest, across some of Europe's most famous cities for food. Book two weeks off, throw calorie caution to the wind and revel in the speed and easy connections that will scoot you around Switzerland and Italy.

ZURICH

Zurich is Switzerland's chocolate capital. Discover chocolatiers for every taste. From old-fashioned family boutiques with trays of glossy pralines behind glass, to pyramids of truffles in Art Deco paeans, to all things cocoa. Not sure how to choose? Head out on a guided walking (and tasting) tour or deliberate over a thick, gooey hot chocolate at the traditional Café Conditorei Schober. Zurich is also consistently voted one of the most eco-friendly and livable cities in the world, and it's not hard to see why. With seventy green spaces, Zurich is geared around being outside and in nature. Head to Zurichhorn for a lakeside stroll or post-sugar-high swim, or tour the tropical greenhouses if the weather's not playing ball.

FLORENCE

5 hrs 15 mins

Beacon of the Enlightenment, Florence isn't short of world-class endeavours, from Renaissance art to the architecture that established its reputation. But Florence also welcomes foodies with open arms and lavishes them with experiences they'll never forget. From the daily aperitivo ritual to intimate cooking classes (gelato, anyone?), this cosmopolitan city delights in sharing its edible secrets. Make time for an *agriturismo* caper (staying in a farmhouse and sampling local rustic dishes) and don't scrimp on the street food. A *lampredotto* (cow stomach) sandwich is a must-eat for meat lovers, or pick up some ribolita – a vegan-friendly, traditional Tuscan soup-stew.

TIP

If you've got a few more days to spare, book in some guided tours of Tuscany's vineyards before heading south.

ROME

1 hr 26 mins

Italy's messy, riotous capital has stepped up and away from the tourist-trap *trattorias* of the past (if you know where to look). A new wave of chefs is reinventing classic Italian cuisine, so expect small plates, hyper-seasonal ingredients, Danish and Japanese influences and much more, rather than just a dogged commitment to pasta, risotto and pizza. However, you can't move on until you've weighed in on one of the city's never-ending debates – where the best carbonara is. If you've overindulged on the wine, pick up some *suppli*. These unglamorous-looking cheese-and-meat-stuffed rice croquettes are restorative kings of comfort food.

NAPLES

1 hr 10 mins

Naples should come with a warning. There is so much finger-lickin' food here, you might want to never move on. With what was once just food for the working classes, Naples has won over the world's chefs with its incredible local ingredients and simple flavours. From plump mussels hauled out of the harbour to the Margherita pizza (head to Via Tribunali – Pizza Alley – for the best), revel in all of the classics in one of its pretty piazzas. Cheese geeks can try their hand at making mozzarella or cruise the city's old-fashioned cheese shops.

TIP

If you have a little time to play with, tick off Pompei and head over to Capri, just over the water.

SORRENTO

1 hr 17 mins — It's worth making the southerly detour to Sorrento, beyond Pompei, to the other side of the Bay of Naples. The Amalfi coast never disappoints and time never seems to matter here. Whether you're taste-testing limoncello, people-watching in the town's café-lined Piazza Tasso or having a sundowner at the harbour, delight in being in the moment. However, you can't leave town without tucking into a Caprese salad washed down with a local bottle of Greco di Tufo or heading out on an olive oil farm tour.

BOLOGNA

5 hrs 9 mins — Heading back up through northern Italy, Bologna is the quiet culinary champion you need to make time for. This terracotta-infused city isn't short on basilicas and food markets (there are street food and market tours), but it's the tortellini, mortadella, Parmigiano Reggiano and Balsamico di Modena that the chefs keep coming back for. Hit the Quadrilatero – a rabbit warren of tiny streets packed with family-run, artisan food stores to stock up on supplies to take home; and restore weary legs with a hearty serving of comforting *tagliatelle al ragu. Journey time back to Zurich:* 5 hrs 57 mins

New Nordic Delicacies

Embrace the tenets of New Nordic eating, where foraged, local and seasonal ingredients are the stars of the show, as you work your way around Sweden. Bookend this super-civilised train trip with a few days in Copenhagen and you've got a holiday you won't want to end.

COPENHAGEN

Home of the infamous Noma and an influence on any twenty-first-century chef worth their salt, as a foodie destination Copenhagen is a big hitter. Its compact, cycle-friendly layout makes for easy exploration and there's no shortage of foraging, hyper-local-ingredient tasting menus to work through at amazingly hip restaurants. Head to Vesterbro for locally roasted coffees, natural wine bars and bistro meals you don't have to book six months ahead, but which you'll remember for ever. Don't miss the Reffen sustainable street-food market either – not all of this city's best food is complex and expensive.

MALMÖ

40 mins Hop over the Øresund Bridge (as in *The Bridge* TV series) to Sweden – this train journey is one of the best ways in the world to cross a border. Malmö has a quieter vibe, but don't be fooled – there's a lot to discover. Fika is the best place to start – Sweden's ongoing commitment to the coffee-and-cinnamon-bun break is commendable – or tuck into the city's dazzling array of lush salmon-and-veggie *smörgås* (open sandwiches). Malmö's pedestrianised cobbled squares, rimmed with tall timber houses, are just the place to while away an evening with a locally brewed beer and a spot of nose-to-tail dining.

Stop by the mouth-watering food hall Hedvigsdal at Malmö Saluhall (right next to the station) to load up on goodies for a train picnic.

TIP

Cycle or walk through Hammarby Sjöstad, a revitalised former industrial district now dedicated to sustainable living.

STOCKHOLM

5 hrs 27 mins

Sweden's capital, actually spread out over fourteen islands, isn't short of ways to make you hungry. From forest hikes to lakeside swims, farmsteads and incredible saunas (pop by the Hellasgården sauna in a nature reserve), the key to this city is to get active before you eat. There is a huge commitment to organic, biodynamic, locally sourced and vegan here, so it's easy to eat clean in one of the industrial, stripped-back waterside restaurants. On the flip side, hot dogs, meatballs and Middle Eastern-inspired street food are still big business. Or go deliciously retro with a slice of bright green Princess cake from one of the many old-fashioned *konditoriets*.

TIP

Stay for a few more days at Lake Hjälmaren, Sweden's fourth-largest lake, where you can bike, hike, swim, fish and camp.

ÖREBRO

1 hr 55 mins Break up the east–west journey across Sweden by stopping at one of the country's biggest interior hubs, Örebro. Get out to the nearby nature reserve created from the old oil port to work up an appetite for some rustic Swedish home cooking. From smorgasbords laden with local, organic veggies and fresh fish to Sweden's famous apple cake, all washed down with lashings of strong coffee, Örebro's a chance to regroup away from the big-city adventures.

GOTHENBURG

2 hrs 53 mins

Star of the west coast of Sweden, Gothenburg, is constantly reinventing what it has to offer. With its young dem graphic, this city doesn't just harness incredible ingredients, it knows how to have a good time. Choose from complex seasonal cocktails in speakeasies, rowdy taprooms with lobster rolls or tastings at the urban winery. Or just plump for a cold beer and a pile of fried herring, mashed potato and lingonberries from one of the famous street trucks (don't worry, vegans and vegetarians are also really well catered for here). Don't miss the nineteenth-century, Gothic-inspired Feskekôrka (fish church), where you can order up a bowl of fish soup at its legendary restaurant, owned by a champion oyster shucker.

Journey time back to Copenhagen via Malmö: approximately 5 hrs

EXPLORE ARCHITECTURE

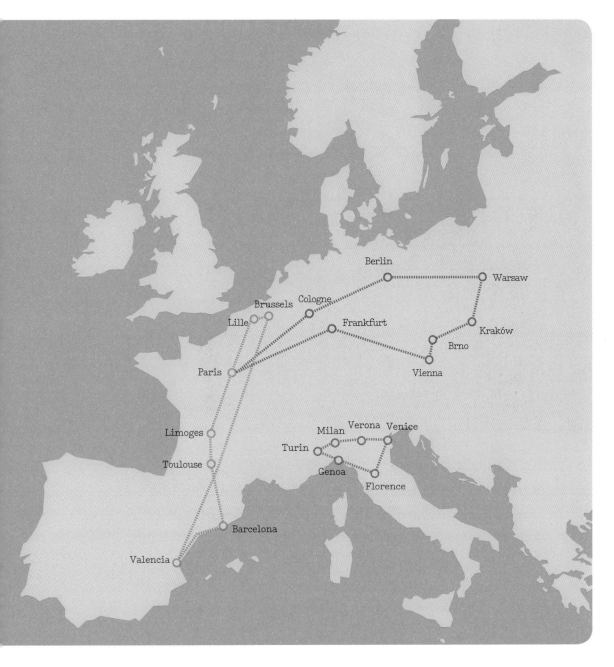

TURIN · MILAN · VERONA · VENICE · FLORENCE · GENOA ·

Italian Appreciation

Really get to know Italy through its incredible architecture in its northern cities on this route. The buildings track the country's fascinating history and its pioneering of many styles, from Renaissance to Baroque.

TURIN

The history and uniformity of Turin shouldn't be avoided; this is a city where a love of art and architecture runs deep, even if it's not flamboyant. A complex relationship with the arts is what you'll find here, among the Baroque palaces turned contemporary art museums (Castello di Rivoli) and galleries formed from empty warehouses, such as the Fondazione Merz. Follow your highbrow adventure into Turin's architecture with a journey to the heart of the Slow Food movement, through Piedmont's famous ingredients like truffles and a Vermouth-based cocktail for aperitivo (the bitter drink was invented here).

MILAN

1 hr 22 mins

Follow in the footsteps of Leonardo da Vinci and head for Milan. It's a cosmopolitan city thriving off abundant culture, high fashion (hit the Golden Triangle area) and contemporary design. Milan Design Week has attracted the world's best designers since 1961. Obviously, you can't miss the incredible Duomo, which took six centuries to build and is home to 3,500 statues, but don't skip the stunning fifteenth-century Renaissance Castello Sforzesco, one of the biggest citadels in Europe. Spend an evening haunting the bars with the hip things in the Navigli District, on the banks of the canals that Da Vinci helped to design.

VERONA

1 hr
50 mins

Journey back in time in Italy's northern medieval town of Verona, the setting for *Romeo and Juliet*. You can check out the balcony of 'Juliet's House' that inspired one of Shakespeare's most famous scenes or book into an opera at the city's enormous Roman amphitheatre dating back to the first century AD. Verona isn't a place for rushing. The pretty piazzas, like Piazza delle Erbe, need plenty of people-watching time. Alternatively, wend your way slowly to the stunning landscaped gardens of Giardino Giusti, where both Mozart and Goethe sought inspiration.

VENICE

1 hr 28 mins Bucket-list destination Venice has more art, history and architecture than you could ever take in, so don't expect to get under the skin of this unique water city too quickly. Venetian Gothic is its own style, inspired by Byzantine and Islamic influences. Start at Piazza San Marco and work your way through the backstreets to the Grand Canal, oohing and ahhing over every palace. Don't miss the Palazzo Contarini del Bovolo for its incredible curved staircase or the Basilica di San Marco, which has an intriguing hodgepodge of architectural styles dating back to the eighth century.

TIP

If you can visit Venice (previously overrun by overtourism and city-block-sized cruise ships) in the winter season, do so; and do also be sensitive to Venetians who are often outnumbered by suitcase-wheeling tourists.

FLORENCE

2 hrs 13 mins Architecture lovers get ready. Florence is packed with must-sees, from the fourteenth-century Basilica di San Lorenzo, once the Medici family's local church, to the Ponte Vecchio which dates back to Roman times. Load up on Renaissance art and architecture at the Uffizi Gallery (many major sites are shut on Mondays), discover how Florentines used to live at Dante's house (Casa di Dante) or the Palazza Davanti, which takes you back to Florence's medieval heyday. Take in the city's iconic skyline at the Bardini Gardens before climbing to the top of Florence's red-tiled Duomo for sunset. It was erected in the fifteenth century and for a time had the largest dome in the world.

GENOA

3 hrs 34 mins Industrial Genoa on Italy's north-west coast is making a cultural comeback. Overlooked for many decades, it's the gateway to the Italian Rivera, but its old town is criss-crossed with medieval alleyways and studded with Baroque palaces. Some of them are so tall, they're connected by hidden paths called *creuze* (which you can explore with a guide). Don't miss the Doge's Palace, an incredible twelfth-century Renaissance palace, now an exhibition space and museum, and tick off one or two of the private palazzos which are now art galleries. Spend a morning being cultured and then rent a scooter and head down the coast in the afternoon for a beer and a swim. *Journey time back to Turin:* 2 hrs

Brutalist Hotspots

Don't crane your neck on this route as we whizz eastwards across Europe and back, taking in some of the most stunning Brutalist architecture. From car parks to incredible high rises, modern-architecture lovers will fall for this adventure, visiting some of the most atmospheric cities on the way.

PARIS

Kick off your Brutalist journey in the Parisian suburbs. While the classical city centre is pretty and low slung, the wider edges of Paris are studded with Brutalist blocks. Start with Les Espaces d'Abraxas in Noisy-le-Grand, which was used as the setting for the final scene in the last *Hunger Games* film, and before you leave check out the double-helix multi-storey car park that will make your head hurt. Don't miss the incredible Viaduc de Montigny in Montigny-le-Bretonneux, which is part bridge, part viaduct and part housing complex.

TIP

Start or end in London and take in modern fortified castle the Barbican, the Southbank Centre and Balfron Tower, a twenty-six-storey residential development in Poplar that inspired J. G. Ballard's dystopian novel High Rise.

COLOGNE

⏱ 3 hrs 55 mins

Despite being a medieval city, Cologne seriously embraced concrete in the 1960s and 70s and Brutalist architecture spans churches, schools, university buildings and public squares. Book a walking or cycling tour to tick off some of the finest examples. It is, after all, home to Gottfried Böhm, one of Germany's foremost post-war, Brutalist architects. Don't miss his Neviges Mariendom (all crumpled concrete triangles) and the Johannes XXIII church, which looks like a deconstructed concrete sculpture.

BERLIN

4 hrs
34 mins

Ah, Berlin. A Mecca for Brutalism. Postwar reconstruction favoured cheap concrete and utility, which means there's a lot to see, much of it away from the usual tourist routes, and mostly in west Berlin. Start with the futuristic-tank-looking, fun-sounding, Research Institute for Experimental Medicine in Lichterfelde before checking out the König contemporary art gallery, housed in a Brutalist former church. For a spot of rare, colourful Brutalism, find the 'beer brush' in Steglitz: a sci-fi-looking tulip-shaped building on a stalk, that's been several restaurants over the years.

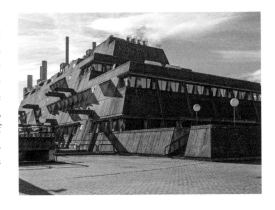

WARSAW

5 hrs
57 mins

Head out east to Warsaw in Poland, and you won't regret it. Poland is awash with communist Brutalist-style buildings, which once promised a utilitarian future of social realism, then fell into disuse, like the enormous Unitra Telpod factory. Many have found appreciation among a new generation, such as the twenty-storey Smolna 8 residential apartment block. There is a range of walking tours that will help you find the best Brutalist gems, but much of the city still exists in concrete and geometric lines, especially around Muranów and Nowa Praga.

KRAKÓW

2 hrs 13 mins Next up, it's south to Kraków. This city has a mish-mash of impressive architecture: while some of it dates back to the thirteenth century and is home to one of the largest medieval squares in Europe (Rynek Główny), it also didn't escape the boom in Brutalist regeneration in the communist era. Don't miss the 1970s Hotel Forum which looks like part of a cruise ship and was once the epitome of high living, and Bunkier Sztuki Gallery, which opened in 1965 and is still a destination for cutting-edge art.

BRNO

5 hrs 51 mins Break up the journey to Vienna with a stop in Brno in the Czech Republic. This off-the-tourist-trail city has plenty of 'functionalist' architecture that will float your boat. It's also known for its 1930s modernist buildings. From the Avion Hotel to Zeman Café, functional concrete design pops up everywhere. There are decent tours here spanning architecture from the 1930s to the 1960s, including some excellent modernist villas. Balance this out with time spent in many of the parks (look out for deer) that encircle this charming little city.

VIENNA

1 hr 28 mins

While Vienna is definitely better known for its commitment to baroque architecture, there was, for a time, a love affair with all things concrete. One of the best examples here is the Konzilsgedächtniskirche Lainz Speising: a church comprising different textures of concrete and an incredible colourful interior with angular pews. Across the city is the parish church, Grinzinger Pfarrkirche, designed as a work of art in itself. And don't miss Kirche Zur Heiligsten Dreifaltigkeit, a stunning block church which looks like a malfunctioned Transformer. Away from churches, tick off the curved residential block Wohnpark Alterlaa. With its lush balconies, it retains all the original optimism of 1960s futurism.

FRANKFURT

6 hrs
36 mins

Break up the journey back to Paris with a stop in Frankfurt. There's a Gottfried Böhm church to discover (the Jesuit Church St Ignatius) and the Deutsche Bahn AG Headquarters – a rare example of 1990s Brutalism. Take a break from looking upwards with a wander around the impressive botanical gardens, Palmengarten, and the colourful wooden gabled houses of Römerberg, which date back to 1405. *Journey time back to Paris:* 4 hrs 55 mins

TIP

Lyon has some of France's finest examples of Brutalist architecture, so extend your trip from Paris south.

Unmissable Art Deco

Into Art Deco or Art Nouveau? Climb aboard for this cross-Europe trip, taking in some of the most impressive geometric lines and flamboyant touches the two movements have to offer. Art Deco evolved from Art Nouveau in France in the 1920s before being adopted by many European cities eager to show off.

VALENCIA

Valencia is home to some of the most colourful and fun examples of Art Deco, a movement that was unafraid to be bold and experiment frivolously. Start with Spanish architect Joan Guardiola's Casa Judía in Calle Castellón and marvel at the mad neo-Egyptian design and bright colour scheme. Valencia was a happening, wealthy place in the 1930s and there are some fabulous Art Deco remnants along Calles María Cristina. There's also a lot of Art Nouveau in town, from one of the prettiest covered markets in the world, Mercado Central, to the Estació del Nord (train station), which will be your departure point for Barcelona.

BARCELONA

2 hrs 40 mins Bustling Barcelona is a paean to the optimism of architecture from the 1920s and 30s. Colourful, elaborate and complex, Catalan Modernisme (a sister to Art Nouveau), wanted every building to be a work of art, the infamous architect Gaudi's work being the best known. Explore his earlier work through La Pedrera Residence and Casa Batlló and if you want to avoid the crowds, skip the La Sagrada Família and head to Parc Güell, which Gaudi designed and lived in. One of the city's biggest green spaces, it's a vibrant place that restores the soul.

TOULOUSE

6 hrs 5 mins Between the First and Second World Wars, Toulouse was a hotbed of Art Deco architecture, with over 200 buildings being constructed, from public instructions to private villas. The Public Library and Labour Exchange are classic examples, while Rue d'Austerlitz and Rue Saint-Bernard are packed with Art Deco houses, all gliding lines and round windows. Don't miss the Piscine Nakache, one of the most impressive outdoor pools in Europe, dating back to 1931. It's like being on the prow of a liner, 100 years ago. The pool is open for swimming between June and September.

LIMOGES

3 hrs 56 mins Landlocked Limoges in the middle of France has long been known as a city that has a strong art and architecture game. Head over to the Rue du Collège to an old refrigerating pavilion for imported meat. It's evidence of the enormous historic wealth found in Limoges that even an old, cold storage building is an elegant piece of Art Deco architecture. It's now an exhibition space. While the Central Market Hall was built a little earlier, it's a marvellous steel and porcelain concoction, still used and loved by locals. Take a walk further back in history via a seventeenth-century fountain at Place Fontaine des Barres and the underground tunnels beneath the city that date back to the first century AD.

PARIS

4 hrs 39 mins

Art Deco was arguably born in Paris, out of the Art Nouveau movement, which started in Brussels, so there's a lot to pack in here. Start out at the Théâtre des Champs-Élysées, the first Art Deco building in Paris, before heading to the stunning Folies Bergère Theatre. While Art Nouveau is everywhere in Paris, from the Metro signs to the gorgeous homes in the sixteenth *arrondissement*, don't miss a trip to the restored Piscine Molitor. It opened in 1946, but it's an incredible Art Deco pool, hotel and spa that makes you feel like you're on a huge 1940s' film set.

LILLE

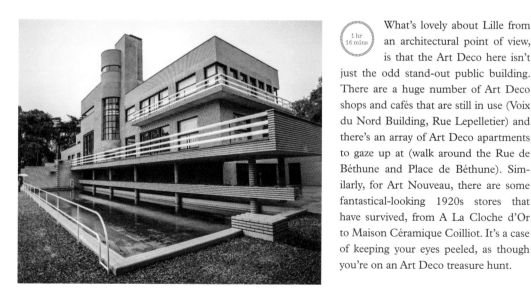

1 hr 16 mins

What's lovely about Lille from an architectural point of view, is that the Art Deco here isn't just the odd stand-out public building. There are a huge number of Art Deco shops and cafés that are still in use (Voix du Nord Building, Rue Lepelletier) and there's an array of Art Deco apartments to gaze up at (walk around the Rue de Béthune and Place de Béthune). Similarly, for Art Nouveau, there are some fantastical-looking 1920s stores that have survived, from A La Cloche d'Or to Maison Céramique Coilliot. It's a case of keeping your eyes peeled, as though you're on an Art Deco treasure hunt.

BRUSSELS

43 mins Birthplace of Art Nouveau, Brussels is very proud of its architectural movement which unfurled from here in 1890, just like some of its trademark curled metalwork. The first Art Nouveau building here was the Tassel hotel, now a World Heritage Site. Tour it by appointment, and call in at the home of Victor Horta (founder of Art Nouveau), which is now a museum. Many of the best Art Nouveau examples are private houses (Cauchie House, Max Hallet House), many of which you can tour by appointment or on certain days of the week. Don't miss the fantastical Maison Saint-Cyr and the Museum of Musical Instruments (which used to be a department store), both designed by Horta.

While there's no direct route back to Valencia, as you're in Brussels combine it with a trip to Vienna (Heart of Europe route, p.82) or to Amsterdam (Picturesque Ports route, p.122).

WALKING
& HIKING

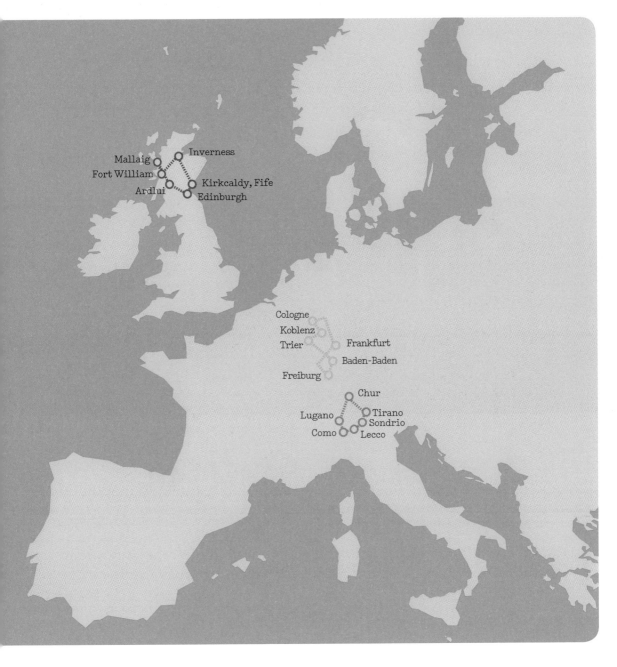

Mallaig
Fort William
Ardlui
Inverness
Kirkcaldy, Fife
Edinburgh

Cologne
Koblenz
Trier
Frankfurt
Baden-Baden
Freiburg

Chur
Lugano
Tirano
Sondrio
Como
Lecco

Simply Scotland

One of the UK's greatest rail adventures just happens to be perfect for hitting the hills, whether you're a fair-weather walker or an all-seasons hiker. From lochs to ancient pubs, this train route is the best way to see some of Scotland's most stunning scenery.

EDINBURGH

Edinburgh's not just about the Fringe Festival, New Year's Eve and the Royal Mile. There is a wide array of walks, hikes and cycles from the cobbled city. The most famous, up to Arthur's Seat, takes you to the highest point of the city (and on a clear day you can see Fife). If you don't fancy huffing and puffing though, try following the River Leith. You can walk beside it all the way from Slateford to Leith (12km) or opt for a shorter distance to the National Gallery of Modern Art (4km), punctuated with local pubs or cafés for a pitstop. For those who like something a little more spooky, Edinburgh has a number of gruesome ghost walks after dark.

KIRKCALDY, FIFE

It's only a short journey to Fife, but it's certainly memorable as you cross over the now UNESCO World Heritage Site, the iconic, rust-red Forth Bridge. The kingdom of Fife (made up of Perthshire and Kinross-shire and Clackmannanshire) is dotted with pretty beaches and easy walking trails. Stop over in the small town of Kirkcaldy to be in the middle of everything. Don't miss Seafield Beach, if you want to spot some more unusual town residents – the seals! You can extend your trip by walking as much of the 188-km Fife Coastal Path as you want to; it takes in ancient woodland and Scotland's iconic home of golf – St Andrews. There are over forty courses in Fife alone.

47 mins

INVERNESS

2 hrs 43 mins   Stern but compact, Inverness sits at the top end of famous Loch Ness, where you have almost 129km of loch-side trails to explore (and try to spot Nessy), thickly forested Scottish glens or no end of guided walks (if you're not confident about heading out alone) into some of Scotland's prettiest scenery. Alternatively, there's a number of short, easy walks around River Ness and Ness Islands in Inverness itself. Extend your trip with some hiking or camping in Cairngorms National Park, Scotland's largest, which is a 40-minute drive from Inverness. Bag yourself a Munro climb (otherwise known as climbing up a mountain), or head out on a much longer expedition, via a long-distance route like the Speyside Way.

FORT WILLIAM

2 hrs 5 mins

If you want scenic hiking, Fort William is the place. Head to the Lochaber Geopark for incredible geological sites and prehistoric landscapes or make this the time to tackle at least *some* of Ben Nevis – the tallest mountain in the UK. You can also mountain bike, golf or ski in winter, if you're the sporty kind. For an easier but extra-special adventure, pick up the Jacobite steam train to Mallaig. Puff out from under the shadow of Ben Nevis and cross the twenty-one-arched Glenfinnan Viaduct (it features in the Harry Potter films as the Hogwarts Express crosses it), before arriving in the quiet fishing village of Mallaig in just under two hours.

TIP

Extend your trip by undertaking the Great Glen Way, one of Scotland's prettiest trails. There are 127km of path, track, canal and loch where you can walk, cycle or camp.

MALLAIG

 1 hr 25 mins

Mallaig, on the west coast of Scotland, can be a gateway over to some of Scotland's most impressive islands, such as Skye and the 'Small Isles' (Rum, Eigg, Muck, Canna). So if you want to extend your holiday, stop here and take the ferry over; or if you're sticking to the route, stretch your legs on the mainland with the Mallaig Circuit Walk from the harbour to Loch Nevis (takes up to ninety minutes) or book a wildlife cruise around the Knoydart Peninsula, keeping an eye out for birds, otters and seals. If it's a sunny day, the nearby white-sand beaches of Morar are perfect for a picnic.

ARDLUI

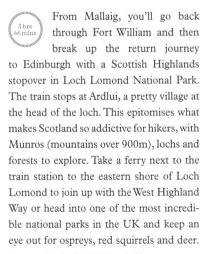

3 hrs 46 mins

From Mallaig, you'll go back through Fort William and then break up the return journey to Edinburgh with a Scottish Highlands stopover in Loch Lomond National Park. The train stops at Ardlui, a pretty village at the head of the loch. This epitomises what makes Scotland so addictive for hikers, with Munros (mountains over 900m), lochs and forests to explore. Take a ferry next to the train station to the eastern shore of Loch Lomond to join up with the West Highland Way or head into one of the most incredible national parks in the UK and keep an eye out for ospreys, red squirrels and deer.

Journey time back to Edinburgh: 3 hrs

TIP | *Hire e-bikes in Mallaig to explore Loch Nevis and the Knoydart Peninsula further.*

TIRANO - CHUR - LUGANO - COMO - LECCO - SONDRIO -

Alpine Ambles

The Alpine border regions of Switzerland and Italy are often overlooked but
provide keen hikers with endless mountain trails, jaw-droppingly
beautiful train journeys and diverse cultures, as they weave in and
out of the regions of Lombardy and Ticino.

CHUR

You can't get better for hiking in Switzerland than Chur, which is surrounded by seventy-four Alpine hiking trails to suit every fitness level. Tackle local mountain Brambrüesch (or take the cable car up to walk in amazing summer meadows) or head out on a culinary trail trek (where you hike between courses eaten at different Alpine restaurants). Surrounding Chur is the dramatic Rhine Gorge which you can explore or pick up one of the many circular walking routes if you've only got a day or so here. Don't miss hiking to the local vineyards, where they have been making Graubünden (the local wine) for over a thousand years.

LUGANO

2 hrs 50 mins One of southern Switzerland's most incredible bodies of water, Lake Lugano, is the next stop on your hiking adventure. This region of azure lakes and bold green mountains is criss-crossed with 830km of hiking trails, beside the water, through Alpine pastures, or up to Mount Bar, the tallest point in the region for a panoramic view. You can also pick up long-distance trails which run down to the Med, or the Trans Swiss trail which is nearly 500km long. After a long day on your feet, relax in this cosmopolitan city's neoclassical piazzas; and be prepared – in this canton, Ticino, they speak Italian, as well as German.

COMO

44 mins Head over the border to Como, which sits right at the southern tip of Lake Como, just 30km east of Lugano. Italy's most famous lake is not just for movie stars or couples getting married – the walks and trails here take in fairytale castles like Vezio or pretty villages, as seen in films (*Ocean's Twelve*, *Casino Royale*). There are over 100km of lakeshore here and you can hire electric cars easily to explore further than you can on foot.

LECCO

1 hr 18 mins Across the other side of Lake Como is the more under-the-radar Lecco, which has a Med-meets-mountains feel. This lakeside town has as a backdrop the jagged Monte Resegone, which has trails for all abilities (or skip the hard work and take the cable car to the top for an incredible view). Just to the south of Lecco is Monte Barro Regional Park, with 44km of trails that take in meadows, plains, lakes and over 1,000 species of flowers and wildlife. Alternatively, you can relax and take up people-watching on the lake – you never know which celebs will be in town!

SONDRIO

1 hr 19 mins It's not just about the mountain hiking in this classic Italian Alpine town – there are fabulous vineyards that dot the terraced lower mountain slopes (it's the largest such wine-growing area in Europe) and red wine is a serious business, even on the everyday dinner table. In fact, wine tasting and mountain sports are combined here in a festival every November. And with tiny, winding streets that uncover eighteenth-century tromp-l'oeil, rustic farmhouses and hidden courtyards, there's plenty here to amuse you if you need a break from the trails.

TIRANO

30 mins

Tirano might be a typical Lombardy town in northern Italy (and as it's Lombardy, if you want one last hike, head out in any direction and you'll hit a mountain), but it's also the start/end point for one of the most spectacular train trips in Europe. Pick up the Bernina Express (book a panoramic carriage seat) back to Chur in Switzerland. You twist and turn through 55 tunnels and over 196 bridges, at more than 7,000m above sea level, all before arriving back in Chur. *Journey time back to Chur:* 4 hrs

FRANKFURT - COLOGNE - KOBLENZ - TRIER - BADEN BADEN - FREIBURG

Walkways & Waterfalls

While many of these routes cross borders, sometimes it's better to use the train to really get under the skin of just one country. Often overlooked in favour of its city breaks, the German countryside offers up some incredible experiences on foot. Trails are well maintained, clearly signposted and accessible.

COLOGNE

Cologne is rich in history, but this region of Germany – the North Rhine-Westphalia – is also famous for its hiking. Seven long-distance trails run through the region, some following in the footsteps of pilgrims (Way of St James) or taking in Roman ruins (Roman Canal Hiking Trail). If you're looking to rest weary feet, there are plenty of self-guided walking tours to the city that include its famous cathedral and both sides of the Rhine. Volksgarten is a huge park with a lake, perfect for a sunny sit down, or there's Forstbotanischer Garten, a themed botanical garden with a Japanese section, American redwoods and a 'Rhododendron Canyon'.

KOBLENZ

1 hr 10 mins Sat on the confluence of the Rhine and the Mosel rivers, Koblenz makes a fantastic base for hikers to explore some of the surrounding forested hikes. You can access parts of long-distance trails, the Rheinsteig (which runs from Bonn to Wiesbaden) or the Moselsteig, which would take you to the French border if you were to follow it for twenty-four days. You don't have to go that far though to enjoy gentle trails alongside the thick Rhine river or discover Gothic fairytale castles poking out from the treeline. Pick up the Rheinsteig in Ehrenbreitstein, or the Moselsteig, which breaks down into smaller circular routes for half- and full-day hikes. Koblenz is a great introduction to Germany's hugely varied landscapes.

TRIER

1 hr 24 mins

Head over to Germany's oldest town (there are plenty of Roman ruins to explore) with a scenic train route that follows the River Mosel west to the border of Luxembourg. Here you can pick up the Moselsteig and Rheinsteig again or explore the vineyards and stunning river valleys of the borderlands, where German, Luxembourgish and French are all spoken (often in the same sentence). There are eighteen local hiking trails or you can take an extra day or so to explore NaturWanderPark delux, where you can criss-cross the borders as you pick between nine circular hiking routes across meadows, rocky streams, ancient woods, reservoirs and beautiful picnic spots.

BADEN-BADEN

3 hrs 58 mins Head into the heart of the Black Forest and some of Germany's most iconic scenery, making Baden-Baden your base here. Deep, dark forests (it's no surprise the Brothers Grimm came from the Black Forest), waterfalls, myths and legends await walkers here. Geroldsau Waterfall is great for families or those wanting an easy life, while the Wilderness Trail in the Black Forest National Park weaves its way over and under trees felled by a hurricane in 1999 and is a fab half-day walk for those not feeling a full-on hike. Restore yourself post hike in Baden-Baden's famous baths, fed by twelve natural thermal springs. And relax.

TIP

Spend half a day exploring Hell's Valley, a deep gorge near Freiburg, which you can ride through on a train.

FREIBURG

FRANKFURT

42 mins The capital of the Black Forest, Freiburg, fulfills many Gothic fantasies, but you can also hike from this town's classic cobbled squares to Lake Constance or the local mountain, Schlossberg (there's also a cable car available). This entire region is dotted with evergreen mountains that will take your breath away, so how many you tackle is up to you. But there's water here, too. Germany's tallest waterfall isn't far away in Triberg and the area is littered with pristine lakes – there are six dotted around Freiburg where you can swim, camp and walk by the shore. Lake Flückigersee also has an area for naturists. And of course, while you're here you can stock up on energy for your walks with the classic Black Forest gateau.

2 hrs 11 mins Break up your journey back to Cologne with a stop in Frankfurt. This central German financial hub has more than just skyscrapers to offer. It is surrounded by the Frankfurt Green Belt: 70km of pasture, orchards and nature reserves providing easy walks around the city. It also includes the Stadtwald – the largest urban forest in Germany. And don't miss a trip to Schwanheimer Düne, which has endless boardwalks over inland sand dunes and meadows for half- or full-day trails. The wider area, Hessen, is packed with yet more forests and mountains. A great place to start, if you're planning on staying here for a few days, is the Naturpark Taunus, with 210 hiking and cycling routes, plus plenty of camping spots. *Journey time back to Cologne:* 1 hr 28 mins

ROMANTIC ROAMS

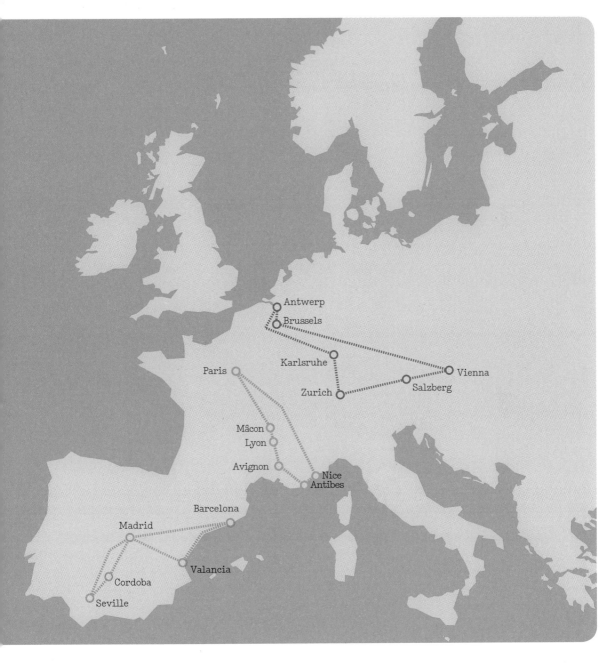

Antwerp

Brussels

Karlsruhe

Vienna

Zurich

Salzberg

Paris

Mâcon

Lyon

Avignon

Nice

Antibes

Barcelona

Madrid

Valancia

Cordoba

Seville

French Flair

What could be more romantic than a slow-travel adventure through France, working your way further south, making time for picnics, patisseries, pastis and *pétanque*?

PARIS

Kick off your French adventure in the City of Love. While there is no end of romantic things to do in Paris, steer clear of the city centre and head for Montmartre, once home to Renoir, Degas, Toulouse-Lautrec and Picasso. Visit the I Love You wall to learn how to say the phrase in 250 languages, go boating à deux on Lac Inférieur at Bois de Boulogne (in the summer there are open-air Shakespeare performances here) and finish up in a classic French bistro. Enjoy a slice of Parisian life and play a few rounds of the classic game, *pétanque*. Find it canalside at Canal de l'Ourcq, a trendy spot where you can also picnic by the water.

MÂCON

3hrs 12mins

Your first stop outside Paris, south of the Burgundy region, is Mâcon – home of some exceptionally good Chardonnays. Use this gentle rural town as a base to start to unwind and taste some of France's best wine. Hire a (low-CO_2-emission) car or book a tour to explore family-owned vineyards, co-ops and *caves* (wine cellars), or take in the lush, green countryside and rolling hills by bike. Wander the colourful food markets, piled high with cheeses, veggies and cured meats and revel in the simple life away from the big city – great food, decent wine and soothing sunshine.

LYON

55 mins It's not far to Lyon, which gets overlooked on the rush south, but shouldn't be. With Roman and medieval history on every corner and down every *traboule* (secret passageways that criss-cross the city), there's plenty to create a romantic atmosphere. You have the UNESCO-listed Old Town, Rhône and Saône Rivers to stroll along, plus the rich, decadent Lyonnais cuisine – and if that doesn't bring joy to your heart, nothing will. This is a city where enjoying the good life is part and parcel of every day. Shop the tiny boutiques on Rue des Pierres Plantées, watch the sunset over the city from the roof of the Fourvière (take the funicular up) and then hit up a rooftop bar (often found on top of former industrial warehouses) next to the river. You'll be smitten.

AVIGNON

1 hr 4 mins

Avignon in Provence makes the perfect backdrop for a slow, romantic adventure. There's the famous Pont d'Avignon (or what's left of it), the café-lined, cobbled streets shaded with ancient trees and don't miss the Jardin du Rocher des Doms, a pretty, romantic park for a picnic (stock up at the traditional covered market, Les Halles D'Avignon), right in the middle of the city. Avignon is a slow, quiet place to spend a few days, but that's part of its charm. Linger over long breakfasts in medieval courtyards in the Med-like warmth, book the secret tour of the Pope's Palace or cruise the Rhône river at a leisurely pace.

TIP

Use Avignon as your gateway to the rest of Provence, explore the famous lavender fields, visit some of France's prettiest villages (Gordes or Roussillon) or head to Arles or Nîmes for Roman ruins.

ANTIBES

2hrs 58 mins Welcome to the Côte d'Azur! Antibes has attracted bohemians and artists for centuries, inspiring Picasso (take the Picasso walking trail to follow in his footsteps and find the views that he immortalised through Impressionism) and many others. Hit the Riviera coast, spend an afternoon on Plage Mala, a hidden-away white beach cove with crystal-clear water, perfect for swimming. There are a couple of decent restaurants here, too, for a rosé-wine-soaked long lunch in the sunshine. Stroll hand in hand through the forested Cap d'Antibes for incredible Med views. Or if you want something more decadent, base yourself at Port Vauban marina for people-watching, posh bars and even posher yachts.

17 mins It's a quick hop to Nice, the classic French Riviera town, where everything feels romantic, soaked with the Med sun and the promise of a better life. Wander the pastel-coloured streets of the Old Town, stopping by the Old Port which is much less 'jet set' than the main strip, Promenade des Anglais. Castle Hill, the highest point in Nice, attracts many couples for its views over the sea at sunset (where you could pop an important question); or for a taste of the A-list life, head to a rooftop pool bar and order up some fizz before booking into a hotel with a hot tub. *Journey time back to Paris: 6 hrs 8 mins*

TIP

Extend your trip with a cruise to Monaco or take a ferry to St Tropez to explore the classic French beaches in the luxurious seaside resort.

ANTWERP · BRUSSELS · VIENNA · SALZBURG · ZURICH · KARLSRUHE

The Heart of Europe

From the coffee houses of Salzburg to the chocolate museum in Antwerp, take in some of the most romantic cities in Europe across Switzerland, Austria, France and Belgium.

BRUSSELS

There is far more than dry politics to Brussels. For a start, it has two museums dedicated to love – the Heart Museum and, erm, the Museum of Erotics and Mythology (I won't tell anyone which one you choose). Follow that up with a tour of the city's best chocolate boutiques, followed by the classic *moules frites* (mussels and fries), washed down with Belgian beer; or keep things saucy with a show at a burlesque club like Cabaret Mademoiselle.

Head to Vienna on the overnight train – this service was brought back in 2020 to help reduce the number of flights.

VIENNA

14 hrs
23 mins

It's hard to find a more romantic city in Europe. Vienna's imperial architecture, impressive palaces and cosy coffee houses make a fabulous backdrop for dreamy walks, especially now the city centre has gone car free. Spend a day exploring Danube Island, with its beaches, forests and fields in the centre of this historic river, and then book in for an evening boat picnic on the river from Hofbauer Marina (the service runs till midnight). Vienna has over 700 hectares of vineyard in the city limits, which you can explore on a wine hike through the *heurige* (pretty wine tavern villages); alternatively, settle down into a snug cellar for a private tasting.

SALZBURG

2 hrs
22 mins

Continue your romantic adventure through Austria with a stop in baroque Salzburg, home of Mozart. In this city of culture, you'll find medieval fortresses next to modern art galleries and ancient squares with contemporary sculptures, so soak up the art vibes from a traditional coffee house (apple strudels are a must). Don't skip the seventeenth-century Mirabell Palace (in *The Sound of Music* and truly lovely) or the Hellbrunn Palace – the best place for a romantic stroll in its huge grounds is between the fountains and the grottos. Top it all off with a lavish meal at one of the historic, chandelier-strewn Austrian restaurants that boast their own string quartets.

ZURICH

5 hrs 24 mins Break up the trip back north with a stop in Zurich. Make the most of Lake Zurich with an evening dinner cruise, hire a paddleboat to work off some of the Austrian pastries or take a ferry to Rapperswil, on the other side of the lake – this smaller city is known as the 'city of roses' and has a stunning twelfth-century castle. Back in Zurich, what's more romantic than a fondue for two in a traditional Swiss chalet (in the winter there's even a fondue tram ride), followed by a hot chocolate at one of the world-class chocolatiers?

KARLSRUHE

2 hrs 50 mins Continue your journey with a stop in Karlsruhe in Germany, on the edge of the Black Forest. Karlsruhe, designed in the shape of a fan, is a treasure trove of neoclassical design. There are an impressive range of museums and art galleries but it's not all about looking backward. Call in at the old munitions factory turned cutting-edge art and technology centre or book a show at the Baden State Theatre, one of the best opera and ballet theatres in the country, before spending a leisurely afternoon at one of the many impressive patisseries.

ANTWERP

5 hrs 15 mins

Back into Belgium for our final romantic stop. Antwerp was once a huge trading port, specialising in fabrics and diamonds, and that rich history is still evident in the grand squares (like Grote Markt) and impressive guild houses. For couples looking to spend a weekend here, there's plenty to do. Antwerp is home not only to a huge diamond museum, but also the largest chocolate museum in the world, Chocolate Nation. Stop for *frites* in a little café on the Vrijdagmarkt, browse the antique shops in a sixteenth-century secret alley (Vlaeykensgang) or find respite in the garden at Rubens House, the seventeenth-century palace where the painter created his masterpieces. *Journey time back to Brussels:* 42 mins

TIP | Chocolate-box medieval town Bruges has suffered in recent years with overtourism, but if you visit out of season and are sensitive to your impact, it makes a great add-on after Antwerp.

SEVILLE · CORDOBA · MADRID · BARCELONA · VALENCIA · MADRID

Spanish Sunsets

What could be more romantic than a hot, slow trip around Spain? From passionate flamenco to hidden plazas, explore Spain's history together, stopping for plenty of siestas.

VALENCIA

Coastal Valencia has echoes of Barcelona without the crowds. Its Carmen District in the walled old town is the place for a long lunch on one of the tiled plazas (washed down with Agua de Valencia, an easy-drinking local cocktail), before you head to the Bridge of Flowers, which spans the riverbed-turned-gardens separating the old city from the rest of this thriving seaside city. Spend an afternoon at the beach – Cabanyal and Malvarrosa are the best – before exploring the old fisherman's district, El Cabanyal, now better known for incredible seafood restaurants and boho bars.

BARCELONA

2 hrs 40 mins Barcelona needs little introduction, as it's one of Europe's most popular cities, but there are plenty of ways to make it romantic and stay away from the tourist traps. Spend your time, just the two of you, taking a private paella cooking class or walking tour of El Gótico (the Gothic Quarter). Get even further away from people by hiring a yacht for the day to cruise the coastline. You can also order a romantic picnic to any spot in the city – and there are plenty, such as Bunker del Carmel – to watch the sunset. In the summer you can also dine under the stars at the Fabra Observatory.

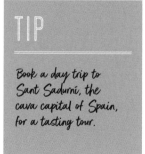

TIP

Book a day trip to Sant Sadurní, the cava capital of Spain, for a tasting tour.

MADRID

1 hr 47 mins

Spain's capital has had a reawakening over the past few years and it's now home to some of the most exciting restaurants in the country (remember the party only gets going at around 2 am). Work up an appetite wandering the cobbled streets of Malasaña, catch the sunset from one of the city's many rooftop bars and head to Platea Madrid, an upmarket 'gastronomic centre', with several floors of modern tapas and street food (there are often flamenco and other performances going on as well). Extend your evening with a visit to one of the capital's many *gin tonic* bars, where the humble G&T is elevated to almost mythical proportions (it's seen as an after-dinner drink here rather than a pre-dinner one).

CORDOBA

1 hr
47 mins

Head south to Cordoba in Andalusia for an exotic mix of Roman and Islamic history. It's hard to believe but 1,000 years ago this was the largest city in the world, known as a centre for science and culture. Be wooed by the breathtaking Mosque-Cathedral of Cordoba, built over 1,100 years ago, and wander through the lush walled gardens and courtyards of the royal palace, Alcázar de los Reyes Cristianos. You'll find hidden courtyards and Arabic architecture in every direction as you explore this beautiful city. Strolling across the Roman Bridge at sunset is one of the must-dos here, as is a hammam in a replica Moorish bathhouse.

SEVILLE

47 mins From Cordoba, it's a short hop to Seville, with its passion for flamenco and opera (*Carmen* and many others are set here). Hot, steamy days call for slow strolls down shaded alleyways in Barrio Santa Cruz, as Renaissance, Baroque and Moorish relics pop up at every turn. Picnic in Parque Maria Luisa (having picked up local supplies at Triana Market) – its tiled benches are perfect for a proposal. Retreat to the city's thermal spa housed in a sixteenth-century palace before your night out. Trawl Triana, which is lined with stunning azulejo tiles for tapas and the local tipple, *tinto de verano*, and end the night with some flamenco at a traditional *tablao*.

MADRID

2 hrs 50 mins To get across Spain you almost always have to go through Madrid. This time, use it as a base to explore the surrounding region. Toledo used to be Spain's capital but now it's like stepping back in time. Start at the central Plaza de Zocodover and see how Muslim, Jewish and Christian faiths have lived here harmoniously for centuries. Or head into the hills to check out Cuenca, a fourteenth-century hilltop village, famed for its hanging houses over a deep gorge. Both are slow-travel adventures away from the crowds. *Journey time back to Valencia:* 4 hrs 43 mins

SKI
DIFFERENTLY

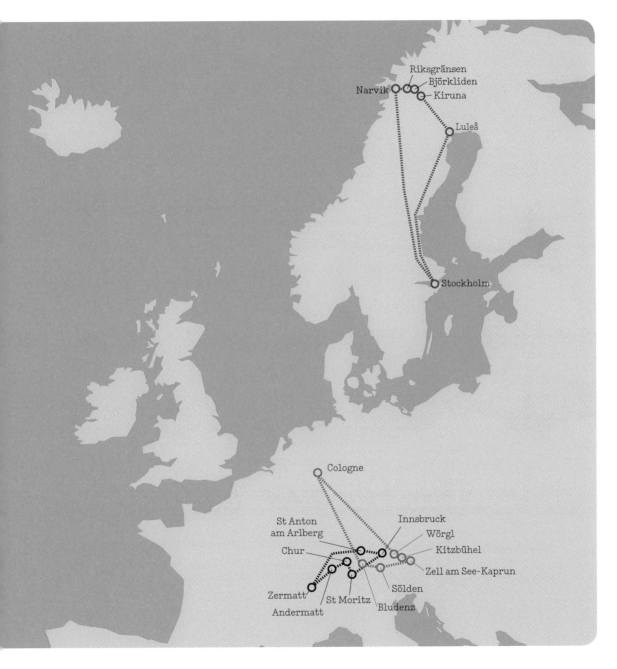

Riksgränsen
Björkliden
Narvik
Kiruna
Luleå
Stockholm

Cologne

St Anton
am Arlberg
Innsbruck
Wörgl
Chur
Kitzbühel
Zell am See-Kaprun
Zermatt
St Moritz
Sölden
Andermatt
Bludenz

ST ANTON AM ARLBERG – ZERMATT – ANDERMATT – CHUR – ST MORITZ – INNSBRUCK –

The Glacier Express

Hit the best slopes Switzerland and Austria have to offer via the *Glacier Express*, which winds through the snow-covered, forested mountains at a sedate pace. If time is tight, head back to Zermatt after St Moritz.

ZERMATT

From Zermatt to St Moritz you're on the *Glacier Express*, Switzerland's comfortable high-speed ski train that connects a range of mountain resorts. Zermatt sits in the shadow of the Matterhorn and is Switzerland's highest ski town with a whopping 360km of blue, red, black and yellow runs. Advanced skiers can take on the Matterhorn ski safari covering 12,500m of altitude; or if snowboarding is more your vibe, the Snowpark Zermatt is the place for you. Ski season usually lasts most of the year, although there are also plenty of hiking and biking routes for summer trips.

ANDERMATT

3 hrs 43 mins

Hop back on the *Glacier Express* and move on to Andermatt, in the heart of the Alps. Wooden chalets and medieval-style timber houses hide cosy *beizli* (restaurants) where air-cured meats and Alpine cheeses are the stars of the show. As well as the enormous SkiArena that Andermatt is a part of, you can try cross-country skiing, with 28km of trails (including a 2km night trail). Don't miss the Après Ski Bar (actually a train) which trundles between Andermatt and Disentis, complete with a bustling bar and DJ!

CHUR

2 hrs 29 mins

Break up your journey on to Austria, with a stop in Chur. Its winter sports' area at local mountain Brambrüesch has 20km of pistes, but it also provides easy access to the much larger and more varied Arosa-Lenzerheide ski region. Book a ski tour of the wider canton, Graubünden – there are 1,000 peaks, 150 valleys and 615 lakes to discover (you can do multi-day tours) across this eastern part of Switzerland. There are also four thermal spas surrounding this Alpine town if you'd like to take a break and restore weary limbs.

ST MORITZ

2 hrs 18 mins The *Glacier Express* winds up from Chur over the famous curved Landwasser Viaduct (sit on the right for the best view). It ends in perhaps Switzerland's most famous ski resort, playground of the rich and famous who winter here to shop the designer boutiques and watch the annual polo-on-ice tournaments. Regular folk can still enjoy this original winter ski resort though. There are eighty-seven pistes here that meet World Cup standards. Start by taking the early-morning cable car to Corviglia Snowpark for pristine powder. Après ski here is a serious (and expensive) business, with the town's clubs known for hosting royalty and A-listers, so it's a great spot to get a taste of the high life!

INNSBRUCK

5 hrs
37 mins

Once you've arrived in Innsbruck you have thirteen fabulous Austrian ski areas to choose from (known as Olympia SkiWorld, with one ski pass for them all). It's your gateway to the Tyrol, Italy's Southern Tyrol and the Dolomites as well. Patscherkofel, Muttereralm and Oberperfuss are better for moderate skiers, while Nordkette is steeper and Axamer Lizum is better for off-piste lovers. Don't miss the futuristic ski-jump tower – the Bergisel, designed by Zaha Hadid – where you can view the city 50m up, just as the ski jumpers do (ski jumping was invented here in the 1920s).

ST ANTON AM ARLBERG

1 hr 7 mins

This charming village is often overlooked in favour of the more glitzy neighbouring resorts, but considers itself to be the 'cradle of Alpine skiing' and it's not hard to see why. The ski area includes 305km of marked ski runs, 200km of off-piste, challenging steep slopes and deep-snow runs, while eighty-eight cable cars link it all together. For a gentler take, there are over 40km of cross-country ski trails, as well as sleigh riding in the evenings, which will add a touch of romance to any trip. If you're looking for something more intimate and traditional, it's worth spending a few days here.

Journey time back to Zermatt: 6 hrs 51 mins

SÖLDEN ~ BLUDENZ ~ COLOGNE ~ WÖRGL ~ KITZBÜHEL ~ ZELL AM SEE-KAPRUN ~

The Alpen Express

The *Alpen Express* has made it super-easy to explore Austria's mountains and ski resorts without having to go near an airport. Each stop provides you with access to a wide network of valleys and ski areas. There is no end of variations, giving you a different holiday every time.

COLOGNE

Cologne, in Germany, is the jumping-off point for the *Alpen Express* which links some of the best ski resorts in Austria. There is a range of sleeper cars (for different budgets), as well as an at-seat service and a pub-car. Spend a night in Cologne, exploring its famous cathedral (you can test your ski legs by climbing up to the roof), and get into the swing of après ski at one of the city's many boisterous beer halls – Rhinelanders like a drink.

WÖRGL

7 hrs
4 mins

Wörgl is your entry point to the SkiWelt Wilder Kaiser Brixental, where 300km of slopes await keen skiers and snowboarders, and local mountain Möslalmkogel sits in the distance. There are also accessible winter hiking trails between many of the nearby villages, which can be self-guided or guided; you can even hike with llamas and alpacas! Nearby ski resorts Hopfgarten and Brixen im Thale are both accessible by train from Wörgl in around thirty minutes – the former gives you access to the 1,829m Hohe Salve mountain, but night owls should head to the latter for a bit of night skiing.

The *Alpen Express* splits at Wörgl, heading both east and west.

If you head east . . .

KITZBÜHEL

40 mins — Pick up the *Alpen Express* again to Kitzbühel, one of Austria's favourite ski resorts. It's home to the Streif downhill ski racecourse on the Hahnenkamm mountain and 230km of pristine slopes. Sixty huts and Alpine restaurants dot these peaks. It's also a great place to try ski touring across the Bichlalm area, with guided evening tours every Friday. Its low-slung wooden chalets with carved balconies also hide a variety of museums, including one dedicated to Krampus, the scary half-devil, half-goat legend.

ZELL AM SEE-KAPRUN

(49 mins) Head to Lake Zell in southern Austria, Zell am See-Kaprun. There are over 400km of world-class pistes between three resorts: Skicircus Saalbach Hinterglemm Leogang Fieberbrunn, the Schmittenhöhe in Zell am See and the Kitzsteinhorn Kaprun. From here, you can access Schmittenhöhe and Grossglockner mountains, the Kitzsteinhorn glacier and the Gipfelwelt 3000 panoramic platform in Hohe Tauern National Park, which sits over 3,000m above sea level. Zell am See-Kaprun also has a night slope you can ski on until 9 pm.

If you head west . . .

SÖLDEN

(3 hrs 21 mins) If you want guaranteed snow, get off at Otztal and pick up the transfer to Sölden in the Tyrol. This stunning resort sits between 1,350 and 3,340m above sea level and has two glaciers you can ski and a snow-making system. All in all, there are 144km of slopes at your disposal. Fill your boots at one of the cosy wooden Alpine chalet restaurants; Sölden is also home to one of the highest fine-dining restaurants in Europe. James Bond's *Spectre* was partly shot here – you can follow in the famous spy's footsteps at a mountain-top cinema.

BLUDENZ

2 hrs
51 mins

At the end of the western route for the *Alpen Express* sits Bludenz, which takes in ten ski resorts, over 1,000km of pristine pistes and 200 ski lifts. This pretty Austrian town is at the heart of five valleys in the southernmost corner of Vorarlberg, where traditions run deep – such as the town still having nightwatchmen who you can join on a tour. Experienced skiers can access the Arlberg ski region via Stuben am Arlberg, while Ski Area Sonnenkopf is perfect for beginners and families.

Journey time back to Cologne: 7 hrs 34 mins

Arctic Adventure

If stepping into the Arctic Circle is on your hit list, this is the route for you. Get ready to take in some spectacular landscapes and try a spot of snowmobiling for good measure.

STOCKHOLM

Stockholm is certainly super-cool, but you can indulge in a whole range of winter sports in the city or get a quick ski in at a number of ski resorts. They are more functional than fancy, but they'll get you in the mood for what's to come. Hammarbybacken is only ten minutes on the train from central Stockholm but it has four slopes; while Flottsbro has five and is twenty-five minutes away. Back in the city, try your hand at ice skating (for free) at Kungsträdgården, or watch others take to the ice for a game of ice hockey, either at Hovet or the Ericsson Globe.

LULEÅ

13 hrs 35 mins (overnight)

Break up the long journey up to the Arctic with a stop in the compact city of Luleå. It has three small ski resorts nearby, perfect for single-day ski adventures. Children will love Ormbergsbacken and Måttsundsbacken, both of which have kids' slopes and sledging. Or head over to Storklinten, where eighteen slopes and five lifts, plus cross-country skiing trails and snowmobiling are on offer. Add an extra night to your visit, and stay at the famous Treehotel near by, spending the night among the stars.

KIRUNA

3 hrs 58 mins

There's one fabulous reason to stop in Kiruna, and that's to see the Ice Hotel, built each year out of blocks of ice harvested from the local river and left to melt in the spring. Each suite (made completely of ice) is themed and features incredible ice sculptures (which you can try your hand at). Skiers can take to the Arctic Circle for a spot of cross-country skiing or snowmobiling or discover how to survive in sub-zero temperatures on a day's adventure course.

BJÖRKLIDEN

1 hr 20 mins Björkliden is famous in Scandinavia for its spectacular views and range of runs. It's especially geared to seasoned skiers, with Sweden's third-greatest vertical drops. Take your pick of 8,000m+ of ski runs. There is also a big focus on off piste here, and the non-adrenaline junkies can try cross-country skiing to remote lakes or ancient craters. Choose from a hotel or log cabins – or push the boat out at Sweden's highest private ski lodge, Låkta. Plus, being this far north, there's the opportunity to see the Northern Lights in the winter or twenty-four-hour daylight in the summer.

RIKSGRÄNSEN

1 hr 2 mins Experienced skiers will love the wild-frontier mentality found at Riksgränsen. Tucked away in the north-west of Sweden, it is the country's most famous and most northerly ski resort. There are fifteen official slopes here, but really people come for the off-piste adventure, with sixty peaks to conquer. Ice fishing, ice climbing and dog sledding are also on offer – you are in Lapland, after all, so take advantage. Ski season is a little different here – from February to late summer – so make the most of the sun never setting.

NARVIK

1 hr

Head over the border into Norway to find your final destination. At 220km north of the Arctic Circle and 1,415km north of Stockholm, Narvik sits at one end of Ofot Fjord and is super popular among Norwegians who love off-piste skiing, mountain adventures and freeriding. Skiers can dive right in from Narvik town centre – there are World Championship runs, guided ski adventures and Northern Lights experiences to be had. And all in one of the most pristine snow-covered landscapes in the world. *Journey time back to Stockholm*: 20 hrs

CULTURAL

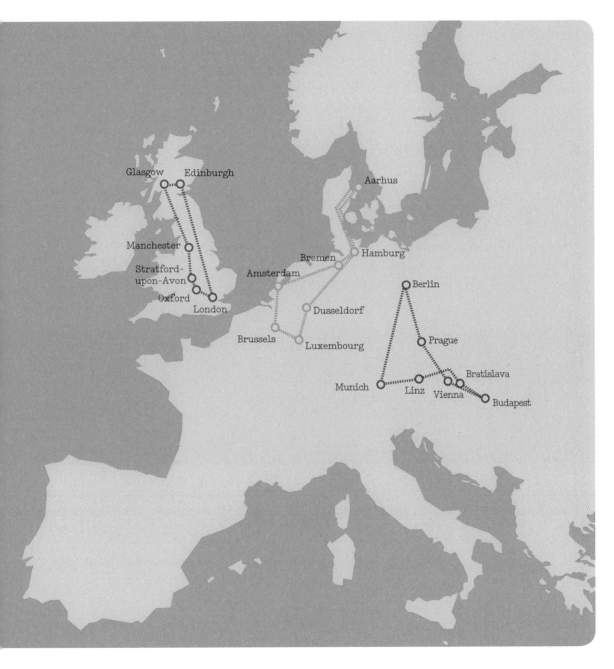

LINZ – MUNICH – BERLIN – PRAGUE – VIENNA – BUDAPEST – BRATISLAVA –

Castles, Cathedrals & Clubs

Take in some of Europe's most popular cities, steeped in incredible history, architecture and art for this cultural whirlwind tour through five countries.

BERLIN

Artsy, liberal, urban, creative – Berlin is a honeypot for those looking to do anything alternative. Tick off the historical sites (Reichstag and Checkpoint Charlie, for starters) and head up the TV Tower in Alexanderplatz before ambling around the street-art-infused districts, discovering the constantly changing artisan cafés, organic wine bars and seasonal restaurants. If you're only spending one night here, you've got to explore the clubbing counterculture. Berlin is home to the coolest hangouts (try Kreuzberg), super-inclusive clubbing, all-night raves and everything in between. Go to Warschauer Strasse for techno, stick to Mitte if no one in your group can agree or Nollendorf Platz and Schöneberg if you're looking for the gay scene.

PRAGUE

4 hrs 30 mins

One of the most popular tourist cities in the world, Prague's medieval Old Town is so incredibly charming, it's hard to do it justice. Don't miss the Charles Bridge and cobbled Malá Strana for full-on fairy-tale vibes, making plenty of stops for hot chocolate and pastries like *trdelník* – a sort of cinnamon doughnut available from street vendors. Obviously, there are castles and cathedrals to ooh and ahh at, but the best vantage point for a city view is Letná Park. At night, start in one of the city's many beer halls that have been brewing for centuries before finding the Old Town has transformed into an alfresco party spot. Skip the tourists for the suburbs, like Holešovice, for more under-the-radar clubbing.

VIENNA

4 hrs 54 mins*

Hit the ground running in Vienna with breakfast in a traditional, heavy-wood-style coffee house and then pick up the Ring Tram. This thirty-minute sightseeing tram ticks off the major architectural sites such as the opera house and Imperial Palace. Join a themed walking/scooter tour (from street-food tasting to romantic hidden gardens) or up your art game by hanging out in the MuseumsQuartier. Obviously, beer's a big thing here; go local with an Ottakringer, which has been brewed here since 1837. If you want the party to continue into the early hours, head to the Gürtel, where new music venues pop up in the arches of the former Stadtbahn railway below the subway.

* or take the night train between the two cities (6 hrs 50 mins)

BUDAPEST

2 hrs 40 mins

Hungary's capital Budapest's layers of history can be explored through its incredible architecture, from ancient Buda Castle to the neo-baroque Széchenyi Baths, a huge thermal-baths complex from the turn of the twentieth century, where you can tick off some history and have a spa day. In fact, Budapest is littered with thermal spas, with 118 of them under the city. Hop on a boat tour on the River Danube to take in the Hungarian parliament and the city's famous Széchenyi Chain Bridge before booking a tour of its famous castle. Those in the know, are aware that Budapest can rival Berlin for underground clubbing, often to be found in abandoned Soviet buildings, complete with communist decor.

BRATISLAVA

3 hrs 25 mins Once part of Hungary, Slovakia's capital, Bratislava, has been attracting travellers for over 1,000 years. It's not hard to see why in this compact city, overlooked by the stunning whitewashed Bratislava Castle. A guided old-city tour gives you a good overview of its chequered history, while the Bratislava City Gallery introduces you to Gothic, Central European and Slovak art. Wash all that good work down with a visit to the Museum of Viticulture, where you can taste some of the 100 best Slovak wines. Book a themed tour to see the main sights (castles, cathedrals, city gates) before heading out on the town. Bratislava's mostly underground clubs (in everything from eighteenth-century palaces to old military bunkers) are monstrous, riotous affairs where locals like to party hard, so be prepared to get sweaty.

LINZ

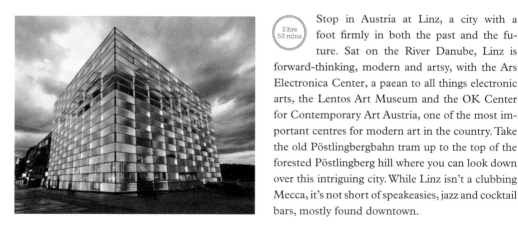

2 hrs 53 mins Stop in Austria at Linz, a city with a foot firmly in both the past and the future. Sat on the River Danube, Linz is forward-thinking, modern and artsy, with the Ars Electronica Center, a paean to all things electronic arts, the Lentos Art Museum and the OK Center for Contemporary Art Austria, one of the most important centres for modern art in the country. Take the old Pöstlingbergbahn tram up to the top of the forested Pöstlingberg hill where you can look down over this intriguing city. While Linz isn't a clubbing Mecca, it's not short of speakeasies, jazz and cocktail bars, mostly found downtown.

MUNICH

2 hrs 44 mins

At the heart of Bavaria, neo-Gothic Munich isn't just for Oktoberfest. With plenty of green space, the city happily balances its hearty traditions of all things beer and meat with its post-industrial architecture and an embrace of more sustainable ways to thrive. Chill out in the city's 'English Garten', which is bigger than Central Park in NYC, and don't forget your swimming gear: not only can you swim here, you can also surf (on artificial waves). And of course, the park has a pretty beer garden. If you're looking for something other than a beer hall, try the famous Viktualienmarkt food market or the Hall of Taste for street food, before ending up dancing all night in an industrial warehouse or hitting the club at the top of the Deutsches Museum. Soak up the drinks from the night before with a traditional *weisswurst* (white sausage) or pretzel. *Journey time back to Berlin:* 4 hrs 33 mins

TIP

Look for twenty-four-, forty-eight- or seventy-two-hour tourist cards in many of these cities which get you free public transport and museum/attraction admissions.

Picturesque Ports

Explore the north of Europe's mainland, taking in political capitals, ports,
the post-industrial and pretty cities across Denmark, Germany, Belgium,
The Netherlands and Luxembourg.

LUXEMBOURG

We will start and end our route in Europe's smallest capital, Luxembourg. The entire city is a UNESCO World Heritage site, but dive underneath it first of all to find a network of casements, or tunnels, that date back to the seventeenth century. They have been used by the Spanish, French and Austrians, all of whom have taken control at some point. Head to Ville Haute, the medieval part of the city high up on a hill, before taking the free lift down to the Grund, a village within the city, perfect for shopping and stopping for a beer on the cobbled streets. Don't miss the Cultural Centre in an old slaughterhouse – host to hundreds of modern-art shows a year.

BRUSSELS

A linchpin for train travel in Europe, Brussels makes a good pitstop for a couple of nights wherever you're going. Having said that, there's plenty here on the culture front. Architectural fans will love the city's collection of Art Nouveau and the incredible Art Deco Villa Empain, a huge mansion–cultural space, which you can tour. Don't miss the L'Archiduc, an Art Deco dive and jazz bar. Counterculture and street-art fans should head for Millennium Iconoclast Museum of Art in a converted beer factory, while art lovers will fall for surrealist René Magritte's former house, now the Magritte Museum.

3 hrs 33 mins

AMSTERDAM

2 hrs

Ah, Amsterdam. The canals, the art, the gorgeous narrow houses and the bikes make for a magical destination, where everyone wishes they could glide around on two wheels like a local. The condensed city centre makes it easy to explore the famous Rikjsmuseum, Anne Frank's House (booking essential) and the obligatory canal tour, all in one day. Once you've ticked off the cultural big hitters, head to the northern side of the main train station, Amsterdam-Noord for a more chilled approach. Don't miss contemporary theatre and exhibition space Tolhuistuin (it has a lovely café terrace), the Eye Filmmuseum for Dutch cinema and the biggest indoor food market in the Netherlands, Jumbo Foodmarkt.

BREMEN

4 hrs
21 mins

Break up the journey east with a stop in Bremen, once a hugely important port for Germany. Its rich history is evident in the 1,000-year-old cathedral overlooking the main square and the stunning Gothic town hall. The Kunsthalle Bremen might not look as fancy, but it's a hugely impressive private art gallery, with incredible pieces from the last 200 years. Bremen was the first place to serve coffee in Germany and the beverage still runs big here – the pretty street of Böttcherstraße was bought by a coffee magnate in the 1920s and turned into an expressionist architectural statement. It's now home to chic cafés and independent shops.

HAMBURG

55 mins

For parks and post-industrial wonders in a port, you'll want to stop in Hamburg, one of Germany's most innovative cultural centres. There are over fifty museums here (don't miss the Kunsthalle for a crash course in European art history) and the Elbphilharmonie, a stunning concert hall on top of an old warehouse, which definitely has to be seen up close. You could easily spend a week here, bar hopping (head to the 'sinful' Reeperbahn if you're feeling brave), museum mooching and flea-market strolling. Spend a morning on the Strandperle, a sandy riverside beach and tour the Speicherstadt – the largest warehouse district in the world.

AARHUS

4 hrs
43 mins

For a spot of serious culture, let's head north into Denmark, to its second city on the north-east of Jutland. While there's plenty of history – from the Viking Museum to the innovative 'prehistory' Moesgaard Museum and the interactive Den Gamle By, an open-air space that recreates Aarhus in different centuries – this is a vibrant, youthful city packed with arts and music and festivals. Don't miss the ARoS Art Museum with its incredible rooftop rainbow-glass walkway. Head to Godsbanen for more underground arts or the Latin Quarter for a drink and a debate about what you've seen.

Stop back in Hamburg for a night or two to break up the journey.

TIP

Don't miss the Infinite Bridge — a pretty circular pier near Varna beach/Ballehage beach in Aarhus.

DUSSELDORF

(4 hrs) An important arts-and-media centre in Germany, Dusseldorf has a quieter reputation than its sister cities but there's no less going on here. With twenty-six museums and over a hundred art galleries, there's plenty for everyone's taste. Try the Philara Collection in an old glass factory or the underground KIT for emerging artists. Otherwise, kick off your art adventure in the Stadtmitte neighbourhood before heading for a drink in a traditional beer hall in Altstadt (beware – the local brew is strong). Stroll along the busy Rhine or take a river cruise (they often serve food and drink) to soak up the city's riverscape. *Journey time back to Luxembourg:* 4 hrs 54 mins

Beloved British Literature

From fictional detectives to following in modern authors' footsteps, the UK is awash with literary sights, writing museums and historic pubs that celebrate some of the most loved books of all time. Take yourself on a journey both north and back in time.

LONDON

From Sherlock Holmes at 221B Baker Street to Virginia Woolf at Tavistock Square, London has been home to a hugely eclectic mix of authors and fictional characters. Kick your author adventure off at Shakespeare's Globe on the South Bank, head up the Thames to Poet's Corner at Westminster Cathedral, where Kipling and Dickens are buried, before finding Peter Pan's statue in Kensington Gardens. Stop by the Sherlock Holmes Museum on Baker Street, or spend the afternoon wandering around Bloomsbury, home to the artists, poets and authors who made up the Bloomsbury Set. There is no end of literary tours and literary pub tours in the capital, unearthing many of the more off-the-wall sights.

OXFORD

52 mins

The historic spires of Oxford have seen a writer or two: C. S. Lewis and Philip Pullman both passed through Oxford University, as did J. R. R. Tolkien. Today, you can pop by Christ Church and Magdalen Colleges to follow in their footsteps (you might recognise some of it from the Harry Potter films, too). Christ Church also has links to *Alice in Wonderland*, as its author, Lewis Carroll, was inspired by the daughter of the college dean to write the iconic adventure. Poets will want to pop by the Shelley Memorial or have a drink in the Eagle and Child, which is where Lewis and Tolkien would drink, discuss books and hand out drafts of their adventures.

STRATFORD-UPON-AVON

1 hr 35 mins On up to Stratford-upon-Avon for a Shakespearian escape There are many ways to tick off Britain's greatest playwright in this pretty river town, from bus tours to bike rides.

Read his sonnets, etched into the paving at Shakespeare's New Place – land he bought after finding his fortune in London. Shakespeare's Birthplace is a museum, but be warned: it's busy. Slightly less busy is his burial place at the Holy Trinity Church which is a peaceful spot by the lazy river, or his wife's (Anne Hathaway's) cottage, 1.6km out of town in the bucolic Warwickshire countryside. Stretch your legs and take in views unchanged since Shakespeare's time.

MANCHESTER

3 hrs 14 mins

From rolling green hills to edgy inner Manchester, stop here to discover the more urban side of British literature. Start at the Antony Burgess Foundation. This provocative author wrote *A Clockwork Orange* and many other culture-defining works. The former mill is an exhibition space, museum and more that also champions new cutting-edge writers. Classicists will want to tour the vast Gothic John Rylands Library or Chetham's Library, the oldest public library in the UK, dating back to 1653. Head to Salford, where radical thinkers have always congregated, from Karl Marx to the poet John Cooper Clarke.

GLASGOW

3 hrs 14 mins Glasgow is often overlooked in favour of the prettier Edinburgh, but the combination of grand Georgian squares and revitalised spirit means that Glasgow can really impress nowadays. From stuffed secondhand bookshops to finding the poems of Edwin Morgan (Glasgow's first poet laureate) etched into the pavements around the city centre, there's a lot to discover. Tour the Gothic Glasgow Necropolis which crops up in many locally based novels, before seeing what's on at SWG3, a riotous arts venue that's home to gigs, poetry readings and a bar.

EDINBURGH

54 mins Hop over to Edinburgh, previous home of J. K. Rowling, J. M. Barrie and Irvine Welsh, among others. There's a lot to see. Kick off at the Writers' Museum, which celebrates Robert Burns, Sir Walter Scott and Robert Louis Stevenson (don't miss Makars' Court next door, where quotes from Scottish authors are engraved) before swinging by the enormous Scott Memorial. Tick off modern authors' hangouts by visiting the Elephant House café (where Rowling wrote the first Harry Potter) and the Oxford Bar, where both modern crime writer Ian Rankin and his fictional detective, Inspector Rebus, drink. Sherlock lovers will want to check out The Conan Doyle, dedicated to all things Sherlock Holmes.

Journey time back to London: 5 hrs 45 mins

COASTAL

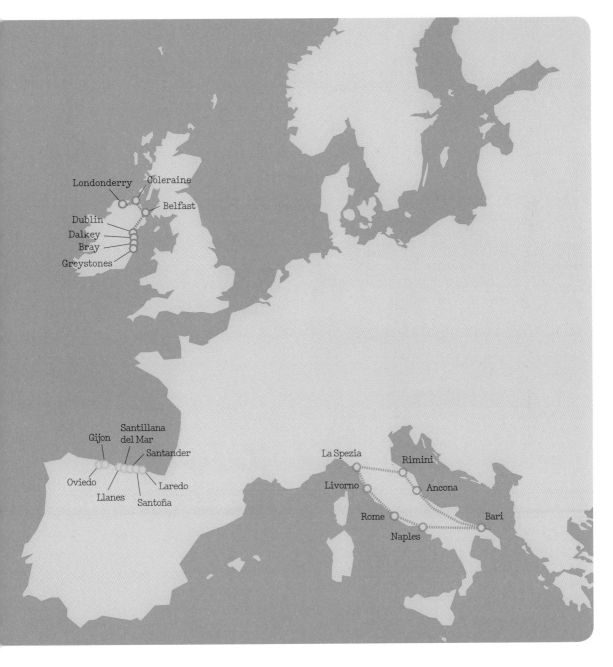

Idyllic Italy

Discover the glorious coastline of Italy, from white-sand beaches on the west coast to the twist and turns of the pastel-coloured Amalfi cliff-top towns and pretty fishing harbours of the Italian Riviera in the north-west. You're heading almost around the entire country on this trip.

RIMINI

Kick off your coast-to-coast Italian tour with a stop at one of its most famous beach towns. Rimini has 15km of white-sand beaches. Head for the Parco Federico Fellini and enjoy beach-side bars, restaurants and plenty of amenities for every kind of beach break. Back in town, stroll over a 2,000-year-old Roman bridge and eat around Piazza Tre Martiri. Set out on a day trip to Riccione, down the coast, for a gorgeous sand beach, plus there are thermal springs and spas here, for full-on relaxation.

ANCONA

48 mins Break up the journey south with a short break in Ancona; Italians flock here for its Adriatic coast beaches. Start with a walk around the harbour, packed with colourful fishing boats, and take in the Roman ruins (they also saw its port potential) before heading out of town to Portonovo Bay, where forests meet the azure sea and wide white-sand beaches. Or head east to find many tiny cove beaches backed by cliffs; this part of eastern Italy is a bit of an undiscovered gem.

BARI

🕐 3 hrs 52 mins Head south and into Puglia, to Bari, which doesn't see the same tourist crowds as other parts of Italy. Exploring Bari's old town and spending time on the town beach will definitely occupy you happily for a few days, but Bari is the gateway to this rich, authentic region with its stunning craggy coast and pretty coves. Locals love Cala Paura for an in-village pebble-beach dip in the small harbour or Cala Porta Vecchia for a sandy beach and safe swimming.

TIP | Use Bari as a jumping-off point for ferries to Greece, Croatia and Montenegro.

NAPLES

(4 hrs 11 mins) Colourful Naples hums with a vibrancy that makes your heart sing. You have the Amalfi coast and Sorrento peninsula on your doorstep – arguably, some of the prettiest coastlines in Europe, full of cliff-backed bays, tiny fishing villages and hilltop towns that cement Italy's reputation for romance. Don't miss, however, Gaiola beach with plenty of swimming potential close to town, and Naples' super-impressive Piazza del Plebiscito, where you can also pick up the local *pizza a portafoglio* – a folded pizza served as street food.

TIP

Extend your trip by heading to Salerno, an hour south of Naples. It's a gateway to the Cilento National Park, which stretches along the coast.

ROME

1 hr 11 mins

Rome needs no introduction, but what to tick off when time is tight? Get off the tourist trail in San Lorenzo, an authentic neighbourhood, where hip bars, family pizzerias and street art jostle for space. Surrounded by seven hills, you're spoiled for sunset views, but head to Gianicolo Hill to look over ancient Rome or Aventine Hill, for a shady picnic spot overlooking the Tiber. Spend a Sunday morning at the Porta Portese flea market before fleeing for the coast. Rome's not that far inland, so hop on a local train to Santa Marinella, a fabulous seaside town with a sandy beach, or head for the Ostia Lido – a proper Roman hangout for when it gets too hot.

LIVORNO

2 hrs 41 mins

A maritime medieval city, Livorno sits at the western end of Tuscany and makes a handy break point between Rome and the Italian Riviera. It's all about the sea here, from the picturesque harbour to the ancient canals in Fortezza Nuova that make you feel like you're in Venice. Make like a local and head out for an evening stroll along the huge Terrazza Mascagni and then dive into this city's incredible seafood scene. Local dish *cacciucco* (fish and tomato stew) is a city speciality. Or load up on picnic goodies at fresh-food market Mercato Centrale and book a day trip to Pisa.

LA SPEZIA

1 hr 12 mins Finally, make your way up to the Italian Riviera, which is dotted with coastal bays and pastel-coloured houses clinging to ancient cliffs. Head for La Spezia and use it as a base to explore Portofino and Sestri Lavante, further up the coast (the latter attracts more Italian tourists and is quieter than the famous Portofino). La Spezia's important maritime history is still evident, but the port is now pedestrianised and lined with pretty palm trees. Explore the nearby Palmaria island, spend time hiking in Porto Venere Natural Park or visit the spectacular Cinque Terre coastline.

OVIEDO · GIJON · LAREDO · SANTOÑA · SANTANDER · SANTILLANA DEL MAR · LLANES

Sun, Sea & Surf in Spain

Get to grips with 'Green Spain' and the north Spanish coast on this coastal journey along part of the longest narrow-gauge train track in Europe (known as the Feve).

LAREDO

We often skip the north Spanish coast for those further south, but Laredo is a reminder of everything we're missing. A huge white-sand curved bay, the Playa de Salvé, extends from this pretty port and the fort-like old town, Pueblo Vieja, which used to protect the town from pirates. Today, it's bustling with bars and restaurants. This is one of Spain's most popular beach resorts, so kick off your Spanish adventure with a few days sunning yourself on the sand.

TIP

Add on a stop in Bilbao before heading along the coast. See p.18 for more on Bilbao or combine this trip with the one on p. 14.

SANTOÑA

2 hrs 34 mins

Santoña is a short distance down the coast, but it feels worlds away from the cosmopolitan cities of Spain. This traditional fishing town is a popular Spanish getaway surrounded by beaches for swimming, surfing and sunbathing. Stroll down the Paseo Pereda Santoña seaside promenade, indulge in all things anchovy (the local delicacy) and remember: drinking and dining start late here. Just out of town, visit the Horse Faro, a dramatic nineteenth-century lighthouse overlooking the Atlantic or head inland a short way to the Marismas de Santoña Natural Park, an enormous wetland and estuary nature reserve (and one of Spain's most important) that will calm and revive you after too much sun or sangria.

SANTANDER

1 hr
5 mins
Capital of the Cantabria region (where you've been for the last two stops), Santander has a lot to offer a holiday goer, even if it's not the most stunning town. It's surrounded by safe, sandy beaches and there are always things happening at Plaza de Cañadío, the hub of the city's eating-out and nightlife scenes. Spend a day exploring the pretty Magdalena Peninsula, where forests and meadows meet the sand and sea. Pick up picnic bits from the nineteenth-century covered market, Mercado de la Esperanza, before you go.

SANTILLANA DEL MAR

1 hr

Santillana del Mar is one of the gems of the Spanish north coast. This hilly, historic town is a red-brick jumble of Roman and medieval architecture. There are no cars and it is home to some of the oldest cave paintings in the world. There is also a pretty, tiny beach at Santa Justa. It makes a great counterbalance to the more resorty towns of previous stops. Stroll the cobbled streets, find a shaded restaurant terrace and settle in for a long lunch (squid is a speciality here).

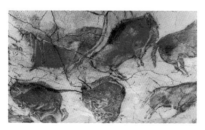

LLANES

2 hrs
45 mins

Llanes is often thought of as one of the prettiest towns in Spain, with a dramatic coastline of cliffs and coves, wide, windswept beaches and incredible rock formations that have been eroded by the shoreline. There are stunning beaches both up and down the coast, depending on whether you want a secluded spot or room for a family, coves, surf or restaurants and bars. Llanes itself is a medieval town that is perfect for mooching around early evening; or try the San Pedro walk – a 1km nature walk along the cliffs, loved by locals and tourists alike.

OVIEDO

🕐 1 hr 35 mins   Head into Spain's north-west corner, Asturias, for lush greenery and rolling hills before spending a few days in Oviedo, the regional capital. It's a city with a hearty reputation for cider, despite sitting on two routes to Santiago de Compostela. Check out the San Salvador Cathedral, where pilgrims have stopped in on their way to Galicia since the fourteenth century. Sip the local cider on the city's boulevard dedicated to the stuff, in one of the many *sidrerías*, and line your stomach with the local favourite dish, *morcilla* (a hearty stew of pork, beans and chorizo).

GIJÓN

34 mins Head back to the coast to Gijón, which sits almost at the tip of Spain's north-west coast. As with most stops on this trip, one of the highlights is the town beach, in this case Playa del San Lorenzo. If it's not beach weather, explore the old town, Cimavilla, with its cute fishermen's houses, dive into the first-century Roman bath ruins or chill out at the lush Atlantic Botanical Garden Gijón – home to 400-year-old trees and over 2,000 species of flora and fauna. There's also a lot more cider here! Mop it up with fried corn fritters (*torto*) and cabrales cheese.

TIP

This doesn't have to be the end of your adventure. You can train and bus it down to Porto in Portugal via Salamanca.

Iconic Ireland

We're going from northern to southern Ireland in this coastal adventure, from the Atlantic to the Irish Sea, via Belfast and Dublin. From live music and craic, to craggy shores and the Giant's Causeway, this trip is packed full of myths, legends and incredible landscapes.

DERRY/LONDONDERRY

Londonderry/Derry is Northern Ireland's walled city and dates back over 1,500 years, so there's plenty to discover. Start with walking the seventeenth-century city walls – all 1.6km of them. Take in a newer monument: the Peace Bridge, opened in 2011 to physically and symbolically join this divided city. The trip to Coleraine is one of the most spectacular coastal train rides in Europe, taking you past Benone Strand on one side (a gorgeous deserted beach) and Binevenagh mountain on the other.

COLERAINE

45 mins Coleraine is your jumping-off point for the stunning Causeway Coast (you'll need a bus or bike to explore it), where the 60-million-old natural wonder of the world, the Giant's Causeway, is the star. It's closely followed by the terrifying spindly Carrick-a-Rede Rope Bridge, 30m in the air, which links a tiny island to the mainland. Nearby Portrush and Portstewart have award-winning beaches and delicious restaurants, too.

TIP

Extend your trip by tackling the rest of the Causeway Coastal Route by bike, where you can also add on kayaking, hiking, sea tours and more.

BELFAST

We have to deviate slightly from the coast, to Belfast. The city's twenty-first-century regeneration makes it a vibrant hub of culture and art, as well as a respected foodie destination (don't miss St George's Market for the best Belfast has to offer). Belfast's cultural revival is summed up in the Big Fish sculpture in the Cathedral Quarter, made up of tiles that depict the city's past. Explore the Titanic Quarter, dedicated to the memory of the fateful ship that was built here or stretch your legs in the leafy Queen's Quarter, home to the Botanic Gardens.

1 hr
41 mins

DUBLIN

2 hrs 9 mins And it's over the border into the Republic of Ireland. First-time Dublin visitors will want to tick off Temple Bar with its trad music, Irish craic and vintage Guinness signs, while returnees might like to kick off with the Museum of Literature Ireland, cycle along some of the city's 190km of canals or kayak through the city centre on the River Liffey. Food-wise, there's a bit of casual renaissance going on, with dishes making use of Ireland's excellent vegetables and organic meat and dairy and Dublin's access to superb shellfish.

DALKEY

39 mins Head south and let the majestic Dublin Bay unfurl before you. The low-cost DART train network links together thirty-one stations around the capital and down the south-east coast and offers up an array of beach, hiking, sailing and shopping opportunities. Stop in Dalkey and catch a ferry to tiny Dalkey Island, keeping an eye out for A-listers who love this seaside town, or tackle Killiney Hill's 153m and find the obelisk at the top, which marks the southern point of Dublin Bay.

BRAY

18 mins
Over the border into Wicklow, sits Bray, Ireland's oldest seaside town (thought to be modelled on Brighton in England). Bray is famous for its cliff-top walk along the east coast (you can walk it all the way to Greystones) and large, sandy beaches. But it's also the gateway to Wicklow's pretty mountain range. Gear yourself up for a hike, and then recover on Bray's Castle Street, where every cuisine can be found, or there are plenty of bars and restaurants overlooking the sea.

GREYSTONES

11 mins
Just a few kilometres from Bray, Greystones is the end of the DART line. It is a small fishing village that now encompasses a posh harbour, marina and award-winning beach. There's a classic Irish '*chipper*' (fish-'n'-chip shop) on the harbour, and there's plenty more here than the beach. Hikers might like to take on Bray Head, a smaller part of the Wicklow Mountains, while cyclists will love the on- and off-road trails that criss-cross the stunning mountains and beyond. Sea kayaking and fishing adventures can be booked from Greystones.

TIP | Extend your trip with a visit to the Sugarloaf Mountain or the Powerscourt Waterfall, both iconic sites in Wicklow.

OFF THE BEATEN TRACK

Slow-paced Sardinia

Swap the circular routes for exploring an entire island instead and head for Sardinia. Climb aboard the old-fashioned Trenino Verde, often called the most beautiful railway in the world. It connects the stunning landscapes across this Mediterranean jewel of an island from June to September and transports you to a simpler time.

PALAU TO TEMPIO PAUSANIA

From the northern point of Sardinia, at Palau, you can pick up the Trenino Verde and travel just under 60km south. Leave the rocky, granite cliffs for arid Med-style greenery, as you trundle to Arzachena, where the landscape is dotted with prehistoric megalithic circles. Stop at Sant'Antonio – Lago del Liscia, for a stunning lake and incredible rock formations. Historic Calangianus, the next stop, is known for its cork products and you'll pass by huge cork forests on your way to the final destination, Tempio Pausania, arriving into a pretty 1930s railway station. The entire journey takes 3 hours 30 minutes.

There are five separate routes that criss cross the island at an average speed of 20km per hour - this truly is slow travel.

TIP Extend your trip with a day on one of Sardinia's best beaches, Capriccioli beach, or you can book a boat trip on Lago del Liscia.

MACOMER TO BOSA

Part of this track dates back to 1888, and in just over an hour, you'll head down from the island's Margine mountain range, through its incredible history and down to the sea. First stop, Tinnura, is an ancient village that dates back to the eighteenth century BC. Discover the island's pre-Roman civilisation – its legacy still plays a big part in the landscape here. Further down the line at Nigolosu, there's the most incredible panoramic view of the Med before you drop down into Bosa, a medieval village packed with terrace upon terrace of pastel-coloured houses that line the Temo river as it flows into the sea. This route takes just 2 hours 15 minutes.

MANDAS
TO LACONI

The retro-looking twin carriages of the Trenino Verde slowly move south down the middle of Sardinia, over the hilly interior, dropping down to the village of Isilli, which is famous for copper on the island. It follows the footsteps of Englishman D. H. Lawrence, who made this journey in 1921. You amble past Nuraghe Is Paras, an incredible tower complex dating back to the fifteenth century BC – the towers dot the island as remnants of its Nuragic civilisation. At Nurallao, get off to explore Funtana Is Arinus, a nature park dotted with waterfalls. Your final destination, Laconi, is a green oasis in the centre of the island, comprising trees, rare flora and a large number of wild orchids. This journey takes 2 hours 45 minutes.

MANDAS TO SADALI

You can also head out from Mandas and follow a different route, to Sadali, taking in some of the wildest and most impressive terrain in Sardinia. The train heads up and over the Gennargentu mountains, past Nuraghe Arrubiu (one of the largest ancient tower complexes) and along the island's second-longest river – the Flumendosa – to a lake between the mountains, where you can pick up a paddle steamer-style boat for the afternoon. With evocative stone bridges, empty oak forests waiting to be hiked, hidden waterfalls and caves to be discovered, this wilder side of Sardinia is like travelling back in time. If you're after a remote adventure, this is it. The entire route takes 4 hours.

ARBATAX TO GAIRLOCH

From the pretty port of Arbatax on the east coast, where colourful fishermen's boats bob in the harbour, pick up the last route and head west inland. First stop is Tortolì, a stunning beachside traditional town that modern tourism hasn't ruined. After a morning here, head further west to Lanusei, through vineyards and forests. From here, it's a walk or cycle to the Bosco di Selene, an archaeological park and thick forest, to discover an entire Nuragic settlement that will challenge your expectations of pre-Roman living. The train twists and curves, working its way higher up into the mountains, through pretty villages with panoramic views before ending in Gairloch, famous for Gairo Vecchio, a ghost village that was abandoned in 1951. The journey takes 4 hours.

Baltic Bliss

Book in a post-Soviet style adventure from Lithuania into Latvia and on to Estonia in this epic adventure. The Baltics are often overlooked, but with vibrant capitals and incredible landscapes, they shouldn't be.

KAUNAS

Kick off the trip in Kaunas, Lithuania's second city, studded with red-brick architecture and plenty of green spaces. Laisvės Alėja, a tree-lined avenue of shops, restaurants and bars is the heart of the pedestrian city centre. Kaunas's architecture in the old town feels quite Germanic, whereas its thirteenth-century castle is more like something found in France or the UK. Travellers who are interested in offbeat culture will love the Devil Museum, home to over 2,000 depictions of the dark lord, making quite a counterbalance to the ornate churches also on offer.

VILNIUS

1 hr 36 mins

On to Lithuania's capital, Vilnius, a muddle of medieval and Baroque architecture. Tick off the UNESCO-listed Old Town before diving into this thriving city's boho scene. Užupis is a left-wing, independent republic within the capital, populated with artists, and it has some fantastic bars and street art. Use the river to navigate this tiny capital, stroll along its banks and take in the city-wide love of street art that has refreshed the former-Soviet architectural severity. Craft beer has also given the city's brewing tradition a revamp; pair a local brew with a *kibinai* – a heavy pastry filled with meat and veg, which can be found at every bakery.

PANEVĖŽYS

2 hrs 50 mins

Halfway between Vilnius and Riga, Panevėžys, is a pretty town dating back to the sixteenth century. Although Panevėžys is on the quiet side, it offers a good opportunity to break up the journey to Latvia's charming capital, Riga. Panevėžys is well stocked with pretty churches that look like ornate cake decorations. Skaistakalnis Park is a good place to stretch train legs and have a run or a picnic, with thick forests to explore. Don't miss the Aukštaitija narrow-gauge railway, which runs from Panevėžys to Rubikiai. Dating back to 1891, it now offers tourist day trips.

RIGA

3 hrs 30 mins

Welcome to Latvia! Riga has rebounded since its independence from Russia in 1991 and in the last few years, the capital has attracted swathes of digital nomads, with its low living costs and easy livability on the Baltic Sea. Medieval old town Vecrīga is worth a wander, with its tiny streets (on some you can touch both sides as you walk along), architecture lovers will marvel at the 800 Art Nouveau buildings (many clustered around Albert Street) and don't miss the weirdly stunning museum, House of the Blackheads, in the city's main square. Riga is the opposite of drab: there's colour everywhere and the whole city hums with vibrant energy.

TIP

Have a beach day on the Baltic Sea at Jūrmala, a short train ride from Riga; 33km of pristine white sand and more Art Nouveau buildings make up this distinguished beach-resort town.

SIGULDA

1 hr 18 mins Head away from bustling Riga to Sigulda, the gateway to the stunning Gauja National Park where thick, multicoloured forests hem in the Gauja river. This landscape is famous in Latvia for inspiring generations of artists and it's not hard to see why. Romantic ruined castles dot the skyline and the air is thick with birdsong. Ramp things up a little with one of many adrenaline-fuelled activities on offer here from bungee jumping to bobsleighing or take on the treetop obstacle course.

VALGA

2 hrs From Latvia head into Estonia, which stretches out north along the Baltic coast, opposite Finland. Border town Valga is a good stopping point before heading on to the Estonian capital, Tallinn. It's a modest town, but there are plenty of quirky things to do, from a winter sports museum to a military theme park packed with Soviet and Estonian hardware. Otepää Nature Park is also on the town's doorstep – this is Estonia's largest nature reserve, studded with lakeside and forested hiking trails.

TALLINN

3 hrs 41 mins Our final destination is Tallinn, another thriving post-Soviet capital. Tallinn actually has everything you want from a city break: lush beaches, a captivating medieval history, plenty of parks (the grand Kadriorg Park was created by Tsar Peter the Great in the eighteenth century) and it's tiny, so you feel like you know it within days. Arts, culture, foodie delights – it's all booming here. The heart of cutting-edge art is the Telliskivi Creative City; once a huge industrial steam plant, artists' pop up shops are now everywhere and the best nightlife is underground, chaotic and decadent. In the summer, alfresco clubs spring up until dawn and more laid-back evenings can be spent speakeasy hopping and cocktail sipping.

Forest Forays with the Fairies

This is a chance to see Sweden as you've never seen it before, away from the cosmopolitan cities and into the wild interior. The Inlandsbanan train is a package trip that you book over six days (minimum), staying in different towns each night. Keep an eye out for lynx, bears, wolverines and elk as you glide through the incredible inland landscapes.

GÄLLIVARE

The Inlandsbanan experience kicks off in Gällivare in Lapland. It's pretty remote this far north and the tiny town is surrounded by national parks, including Stuor Muorkke national park, which is home to glaciers and reindeer. The town is 100km north of the Arctic Circle, and in the summer the sun never sets. Explore the Sami way of life or tack on a visit to Kiruna, famous for the Ice Hotel that is built each winter, only to melt away each spring.

TIP | Extend your trip by travelling to starting point Gällivare by train from London, via hip west-coast city, Gothenburg.

JOKKMOKK

2 hr 51 mins

Dive deeper into the Sami culture in Swedish Lapland, with a stop in Jokkmokk, which has become a centre for traditional crafts, with tin being a speciality. Jokkmokks Tenn is the place to pick up souvenirs, while the Sami museum, Ájtte, is a must visit. The Sami people have used this small village as an annual meeting spot for hundreds of years and the landscape thrums with centuries of shared experience. Food isn't forgotten here either – now's the chance to try reindeer, Arctic fish and foraged berries. Or cloudberry jam, anyone? If you love being outside, this is a stunning playground in summer or winter.

VILHELMINA

5 hrs
50 mins

The journey through to Vilhelmina on the southern border of Lapland literally heads down the central spine of Sweden. Myths and legends run strong within this wooden, low-slung town. Explore some of them by hiking the Sagavägen fairy-tale trail or the Vildmarksvägen wilderness trail, find impressive waterfalls and discover the eternal Sami meeting place, Fatmomakke. Again, most life takes place outside, among the forests and valleys, and it's incredibly refreshing.

ÖSTERSUND

4 hrs Further south into Sweden, your next stop is Östersund. This lakeside inland city attracts plenty of Scandinavians on holiday every summer. Stop here for a day or two of wild swimming, kayaking and some sauna time or stay on and hike and camp to your heart's content. Get further afield at Wild Jämtland, a nature reserve where you can stay in hideouts to watch brown bears and other wildlife make their way through the landscape.

SUNDSVALL

2 hrs 37 mins

End your Scandinavian escape by the sea on Sweden's east coast at Sundsvall in the Medelpad province. A compact, pretty coastal town, Sundsvall is backed by incredible Swedish landscapes where you can indulge your foraging and hiking dreams, but ultimately come back to semi urban luxury at night. Hikers, don't miss the UNESCO World Heritage Site of Höga Kusten, for incredible granite cliffs jutting proudly from the sea. Sundsvall is also the starting point for the northernmost pilgrim trail in the world, St Olavsleden, which runs all the way to Trondheim in Norway.

FAMILY FUN

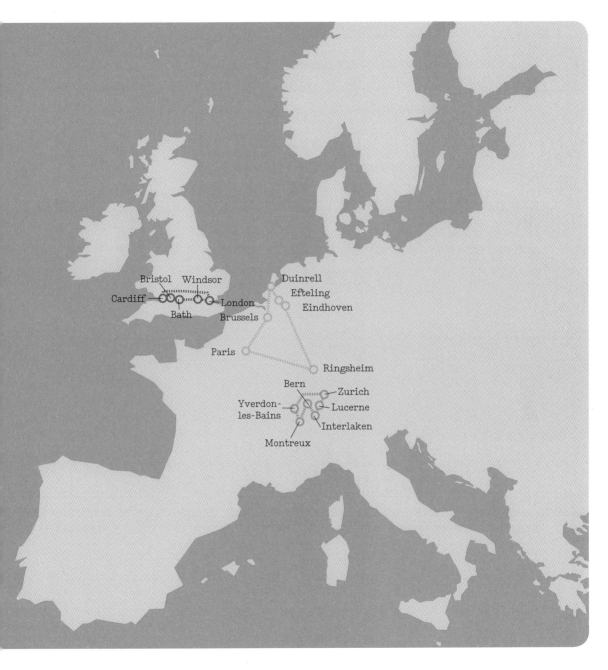

 CARDIFF · LONDON · WINDSOR · BATH · BRISTOL

Legendary Landmarks

Kids are well catered for when touring British cities, from taking in ancient castles steeped in myths and legends to burning off energy at adventure parks. Head south-west and discover some of Britain's history, culture, arts and best green spaces.

LONDON

Make London all about the stories. Stratford's Children's Story Centre is a fantastic interactive experience where kids' imaginations are brought to life. Journey through story worlds and find hidden pirate ships, creep through haunted caves and explore fairy castles. There's a lovely adventure playground as well to enjoy. Keep the magic levels high with a Harry Potter walking tour and end up at platform 9¾ at King's Cross station (just before you set out on your train journey).

WINDSOR

38 mins While many adults love Windsor for the pomp and ceremony and connection to the royal family, kids love the castle and Windsor's handy location for Legoland, which is a short bus ride away. Stay the night and explore both Legoland and Duplo Valley (for younger kids); there are some really charming experiences here beyond the obvious rides and rollercoasters. An enormous miniature cityscape will make adult Lego fans green with envy, while kids can get stuck into making their own movies or playing in the water garden.

BATH

 1 hr 46 mins

Home of Jane Austen and the ancient Roman Thermae Baths, elegant Bath has a lot going for it for an overnight visit. There are often dressed-up actors at the original Roman Baths to get kids interested in the history and the town is awash with museums geared towards families. Learn how to blow glass or head to the Royal Mint, where all British money is made. For something more active, the Skyline Walk circles the city with almost 10km of pretty pathways, perfect for picnicking and kite flying.

TIP

If you've got older kids you could cycle to Bristol on the stunning Bristol to Bath path. It's 20km of flat cycle lanes, dotted with riverside pubs.

BRISTOL

12 mins — Bristol's a city that is packed with alternative culture and incredible plant-based and organic restaurants and its anything-goes energy is infectious. But it's also really well geared for families, from feeding the animals at Windmill Hill City Farm to exploring the Brunel's SS *Great Britain*, the world's first great ocean liner. We The Curious is a fantastic interactive science discovery centre; or you can head slightly north of the city to find a high-flying treetop adventure park. Bristol is one of the best cities for cycling as well, so get everyone on two wheels and head to one of the many parks and trails to burn off some energy.

CARDIFF

48 mins — Stretch your legs with a walk down to Cardiff Bay, a bustling space with plenty of cafés and restaurants, where you can take in the restored industrial harbour. Go on to the Cardiff Bay Wetlands Nature Reserve, where kids can discover a greener side to the city. Tick off Cardiff Castle (there are kids' audio tours, an animal trail and often re-enactments aimed at children) or, if it's raining, head to the Cardiff Story Centre where kids can let their imaginations run riot. Blow the cobwebs away before you head back to London by renting bikes and covering the first few kilometres of the stunning Taff Trail, alongside the River Taff, from Cardiff's green jewel in the crown, Bute Park. *Journey time back to London:* 1 hr 51 mins

Thrill-seekers' Dream

Get that adrenaline pumping with this tour of Europe's best theme parks. From once-in-a-lifetime big hitters to the smaller parks that offer something more innocent, pick and choose your excitement levels and get going. The kids will love you for ever (well, until the holiday is over!).

PARIS

Hold on to your hats – this is going to be a full-on family adventure, kicking off at Disneyland Paris. With fifty rides, fifty restaurants, eight hotels and five 'magical lands' under the watchful eye of the iconic Sleeping Beauty castle, this is every kid's dream holiday. Meet your favourite Disney characters, hoist the mainsail with the Pirates of the Caribbean and investigate Indiana Jones and the Temple of Peril. There's obviously enough going on to keep you here for weeks, but it's never been easier to get here – there are Eurostar services that deliver you straight to the park's magic doors.

RINGSHEIM

4 hrs 11 mins While Disneyland might be the best-known of the theme parks here, there is no shortage of incredible places for the kids right across Europe. Next up is Europa Park, on the German/French/Swiss border. Head for Strasbourg, then Ringsheim, and the park is a short bus transfer from there. Inside, you'll find adrenaline-inducing rollercoasters, fairy-tale lands, gentle boat rides and enough attractions for your kids and your own inner child, too. What's more, it's quieter and arguably prettier than Disneyland, and cheaper as well.

EINDHOVEN

Over in the Netherlands is Toverland, which has pop-up camping available every summer. If you're looking for something non-global branded, Toverland is an innocent haven of six lands, based randomly on Austrian folklore, Merlin and a sunny harbour town. From rollercoasters and interactive rides to magic shows and areas where you can just chill out and sunbathe, Toverland is a laid-back, low-key theme park that will still keep teenagers and toddlers happy. To get there, it's a short bus ride from Eindhoven.

9 hrs 31 mins

EFTELING

54 mins Head on up through the Netherlands to the country's biggest theme park, Efteling. Again, it's charmingly independent and free from any well-known cartoons, which makes it feel like you're going back in time. Get lost in the Fairytale Forest, with statues from a range of famous tales, try a number of 'dark rides' where you can scare yourself silly in haunted castles and cursed villas, head into the clouds in a Thai pavilion that goes up to 45m in the air or kick back on the steam train. There's no need to rush either, as there is a range of accommodation options here, including hotels and holiday houses, as well as low-allergen, grass-roofed villas.

DUINRELL

2 hrs 42 mins

Forget the massive, impersonal theme parks that take weeks to get across on foot – Duinrell is a charming Dutch holiday park that combines rollercoasters and over forty other attractions with a lovely forested green space where you can camp or stay in safari-style lodges. Plus, it has a decent-sized water park with twenty-one slides and a huge, shallow play area for the very young ones. Hire bikes, explore the hiking trails, book a round of mini golf and spend the evening enjoying the on-site pubs and restaurants. This is a more relaxed experience with enough to do for everyone to enjoy their own thing.

BRUSSELS CENTRAL

3 hrs 10 mins

Just thirty minutes from Brussels Central lies Belgium's biggest theme park, Walibi. Famous on the continent, Walibi has huge, scary rides and 4D adventures as well as gentle experiences for tiny kids, plus pony rides and plenty of space to run around. And there's now Aquaibi as well – a huge water park next door (both are accessible from the park's own train station) with wave pools, slides, a mini beach and a kids' play area and pool. There's lots of accommodation near by, rather than on site, and definitely enough here for a couple of days' exploring. *Journey time back to Paris:* 1 hr 34 mins

Scenic Switzerland

Not only does Switzerland have some of Europe's most stunning scenery,
it also makes it super-easy to explore by rail, with intercity trains set up
for kids with jungle gyms, entertainment and activities on board.
Buy a family rail pass and head out on this loop.

ZURICH

Kick off your Swiss adventure in Zurich, which is actually really well set up for families. River cruises are a great introduction to the city for those with little legs, while the Fondue Tram (which serves you fondue as you pass by the main sights) will appeal to the young and young at heart. There are fifteen museums suitable for kids, where they can explore everything from football to science experiments. And pack your swimmers because just half an hour away is Alpamare – the biggest indoor water park in Europe with four pools, twelve slides, lazy rivers (plus sauna, steam and massages for adults). The thermal water is said to cure all kinds of ailments, too.

LUCERNE

50 mins Go south to characterful Lucerne, a medieval town on the edge of Lake Lucerne. Head up on old-fashioned cable cars and funiculars to one of the many mountains that surround Lucerne. There are also masses of adventure trails for kids, a summer toboggan run over a kilometre long, ziplines and plenty of mountaintop playgrounds. While it doesn't sound the most exciting, the Swiss Museum of Transport shows how to engage kids, with treasure trails and detective games via a phone app, plus there's a seriously impressive planetarium.

INTERLAKEN

1 hr 51 mins

Make pretty Interlaken your base to discover central Switzerland. It sits between Lake Thun and Lake Brienz, surrounded by picture-postcard valleys, forests and meadows. Switzerland has no end of outside adventures for kids and Seilpark Interlaken will test older kids with an incredible treetop adventure course. There are 120 challenges over nine courses for people of all ages. And forty-five minutes away, at the other end of the lake, is the Swiss Open Air Museum, where kids can discover what life was like in medieval Switzerland, and try their hands at various crafts at this huge re-enactment village.

BERN

54 mins Stop at Bern and spend a day at the city's bear park. The long-standing tradition of raising bears in Bern (sadly, originally for fighting) has been brought into the twenty-first century here, where this small but impressive park focuses on conservation instead. Head out on the city's Schwarzsee Witch's Trail, a lakeside adventure trail where kids can discover local legends and find the odd dragon or two hidden among the trees. Twenty minutes from Bern is Thun, which has a noteworthy toy museum.

MONTREUX

1 hr 36 mins You're here in Montreux for one thing really – the chocolate train. This family-fun day out takes you from Montreux to the Cailler-Nestlé chocolate factory in Broc. It's a full-on chocolate-tasting adventure, via an old-fashioned 1915 vintage train which also stops at the famous Gruyère cheese factory (so you can balance out all that sugar). Kids will love visiting a real-life chocolate factory, especially one that turns out such exceptional Swiss chocolate.

YVERDON-LES-BAINS

1 hr 5 mins

Work off some of the sugar high as you make your way slowly back to Zurich via Yverdon-les-Bains on the southern shore of Lake Neuchâtel. The pretty spa town has attracted people for 1,500 years, and it's not hard to see why. Relax on the gentle sand beach, kids can swim in the lake (or hire pedal boats and paddleboards) or stretch your legs at Grande Cariçaie, the biggest lakeside nature reserve in Switzerland. A local train takes you to the Pro Natura Centre Champ-Pittet, which has plenty of kids' activities and is a base for trails and guided tours. *Journey time back to Zurich:* 1 hr 48 mins

ADVENTURE

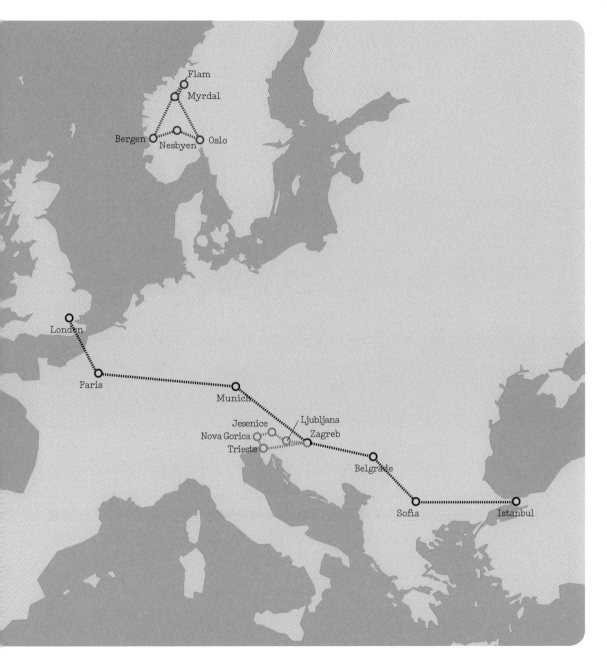

Ain't No Mountain High Enough

Tick off the vast wilderness and incredible mountains of Norway on this adventurous route. You can start and finish in the Norwegian capital, but this ain't no city break: you'll be exploring nearby towns accessible only by train, having a go at everything from skiing to ziplining.

OSLO

Kickstart your Norwegian adventure in Norway's capital, Oslo. Spend a day on the forested Bygdøy peninsula, where most of the city's museums can be found. Explore Norway's impressive maritime history through the Viking Ship Museum and the Fram Museum (which celebrates local polar explorers of 100 years ago). Art lovers will adore Frogner Park, which is home to over 200 sculptures by Gustav Vigeland. Spend an evening at Aker Brygge, a revitalised harbour surrounded by restaurants, then work off your meal with a stroll around Tjuvholmen Sculpture Park with pieces from Anish Kapoor and Antony Gormley.

MYRDAL

4 hrs 45 mins

The centrepiece of this route is the Flåm Railway, one of the most stunning train journeys in the world. The jumping-off point is Myrdal, which is only accessible by train and acts as a gateway for exploring the 'real' Norway and its fjords. Book a tour from one to five days to explore the impressive waterways – you can access Sognefjord, Norway's longest and deepest, or UNESCO-protected Nærøyfjord. And you don't just have to look at the fjords – there's kayaking, stand-up paddleboarding and other water sports too.

FLÅM

1 hr The Flåm Railway is only 32km long, but it takes in twenty tunnels, drops over 800m from Myrdal in the mountains to sea-level Flåm and is one of the steepest railways in the world. Over the course of an hour, it takes in waterfalls, vertigo-inducing drops, hairpin bends and almost every minute offers up an incredible view of western Norway. (Board early to get the best seats for photos – the first and last windows in each carriage open). It's no wonder it's been rated one of the world's best train experiences. From Flåm there are more fjords to cruise, mountains to climb and there's an award-winning brewery to unwind in. Stay a few days in a traditional timber house and breathe in that clear and crisp Norwegian air.

MYRDAL

1 hr Head back to Myrdal on the Flåm Railway, this time climbing back up to the mountains (and check out the views you missed on the way down). Stop a night or two in Myrdal (there are incredible mountain-bike and hiking trails around) or, if you're here in winter, ski to your heart's content. An hour away on the train lies Voss, a tiny town packed with adrenaline-sports options all year round. In winter, there are some fabulous cross-country ski trails, but whatever the month, get the cable car up over 800m to Hangurstoppen and take in the panoramic views.

BERGEN

2 hrs Next up is Norway's fragmented west coast and Bergen. The colourful timber houses feel like something from a fairy tale and there's an edge-of-the-world feel here. Use Bergen as your base to tick off some seriously cool adventures. There's glacier trekking, white-water rafting, ziplining – Norwegians have thought of every possible way to use the incredible fjords and mountains that surround Bergen. It's also the gateway to more fjords, which remain untouched by humankind and superbly peaceful. There are waterfalls to ooh and ahh over and mountains to tackle.

NESBYEN

4 hrs 29 mins

Break the train journey east and back to Oslo in Nesbyen. This charming, small town is a fantastic way to see what rural mid-country Norway looks like (and has looked like for hundreds of years). Mountain biking is big business here and there is no end of mountain and for-ested trails to head out on, and plenty of impressive waterfalls to hike to if biking isn't your thing. The ones at Hallingdal Museum are particularly fierce. In summer, you can swim and stand-up paddleboard on the Hallingdalselva, the long, thin river that runs next to the town. *Journey time back to Oslo:* 2 hrs 56 mins

Living the Wild Life

Take in some of the best bits of the Balkans with this adventurous route from Slovenia to Croatia, via Italy. From incredible steam trains to emerald rivers, mysterious cities to city-centre kayaking – it's all here.

LJUBLJANA

Slovenia's capital should be better known among Western tourists – but delight in the fact that it isn't! Compact, cute and laced with waterways, it's both laid back and vibrant, thanks to it being a big university hub. Ljubljana is a hugely green city, so hire bikes and explore the surrounding woods, canoe through the city centre or hit the local river's rapids, via a variety of water sports. Mountain bikers will love nearby Ljubljana Bike Park with its forested trails or pick up one of the many hiking trails that start in the city and soon get you deep into the pristine Slovenian countryside.

JESENICE

1 hr 31 mins

In Jesenice, pick up the famous steam train on the Bohinj Railway to Nova Gorica. In just a couple of hours, it heads through twenty-eight tunnels and over sixty-five bridges (one of which is the longest stone bridge in the world), all built around the turn of the twentieth century. There's a museum car where you get a guided history tour of the region and the railway as it chugs past Lake Bled (the most famous spot in Slovenia) and Kanal, a small settlement on the River Soča, which is a bright emerald green. The river is used for all manner of sports including 'wild-water kayaking'. Get off and explore these points and then reboard another train – they are definitely worth your time.

NOVA GORICA

1 hr 50 mins The Bohinj Railway ends in Nova Gorica, which straddles the Italian border (head to Europe Square and you can stand with a foot in either country). Here, you've got both wine country and the Alps on hand, where there is also paragliding and hang-gliding. Test yourself with bungee jumping off the impressive Solkan Bridge (with the longest stone arch in the world) or if that's all a bit much, the Vipava Valley produces famous Slovenian wines and there are endless vineyards open for tastings and tours. This area of Slovenia is known for its gastronomy, with prosciutto and goat's cheese being local specialities.

TRIESTE

2 hrs
9 mins

After a well-fed break in Nova Gorica, head on into Italy to the port of Trieste, which sits on a sliver of Italian land between Slovenia and the Adriatic. It's a true melting pot of cultures having been Austrian–Hungarian, Slovenian, Italian and even ancient Greek. Writers have felt its mysterious pull for centuries (spot the many plaques and statues to various authors). Twenty minutes out of town is the Grotta Gigante, a huge underground cave network, thought to be the world's largest until 2010. Tick that off and the Miramare Castle, a grand white palace with pretty, formal gardens, created for a Hapsburg archduke and overlooking the sea. To reach Zagreb, you must head back to Ljubljana. Either hop straight on the next train or spend an afternoon picnicking at Tivoli Park or a night dining riverside before continuing your journey. To reach Zagreb, trains seem to be patchy (at time of writing). Your best bet is the Flexibus via Poreč.

ZAGREB

5 hr 55 mins

Croatia's Gothic-style capital, Zagreb, is less explored than its coastal party towns and islands but it makes for a great adventure. Within the city, don't miss the unusual Museum of Broken Relationships, dedicated to lost loves and broken hearts. Lake Jarun can provide a fun day trip, where you can swim and paddleboard (in the summer, there are beachside clubs that go on until the small hours) or the local Mount Medvednica offers hiking and biking and is also a huge nature reserve. Top up energy levels in Donji Grad (the lower town) where most of the city's bars and restaurants are.

TIP

Continue the adventure by taking the train to Budapest (but be warned – it takes nine to ten hours) or head to the Croatian coast, to Split, via a night train.

Your Own Orient Express

Follow the route of the iconic *Orient Express* from London to Istanbul.
Although the famous train no longer runs, you can recreate the route
yourself. Some of the distances here are longer than on the other routes,
but crossing the entire continent of Europe is the point.

LONDON

Kick off your cross-European adventure at the British Museum to get the historical juices flowing. Look out for Turkish silver, the Lampsacus Treasure, dating back to the sixth century BC. Stock up on train supplies at Exmouth Market in Clerkenwell or pick up any last bits of shopping at Coal Drops Yard, the huge new retail and restaurant development behind King's Cross station. If you've time to spare, take a narrow-boat ride up and down Regent's Canal; it's amazing to see how much this part of London has changed.

PARIS

2 hrs 18 mins

If you're only spending a night or two in Paris, make it count. Take a romantic Seine walk along the river between Pont Neuf and Pont Alexandre III on the right bank. Rent a couple of bikes or e-scooters and tour the courtyard of the Louvre and the gorgeous Jardin des Tuileries, which has been here since the 1500s. Later on, make your way to Le Marais, the hippest area for food, wine and cocktails, and also home to Paris' oldest covered market, Marché des Enfants Rouges, to stock up on some French goodies. Make your way to Paris Gare de l'Est for the train to Munich.

MUNICH

5 hrs 44 mins Break up the journey with a few days in Bavarian capital Munich. Shake off sitting still on the train at Müllersches Volksbad, a gorgeous Art Deco public pool built in 1901 – it's like swimming in a ballroom. Spoil yourself with a massage or a drink poolside. Coffee and cake are an institution here, so linger in a traditional café with cream-laden tortes and lashings of coffee. If you want to get out of town, book a day trip to see Bavarian castle Schloss Nymphenburg – a rather imposing affair with beautiful gardens. Pick up supplies for the train to Croatia at indoor food market, Viktualienmarkt, supplied by Bavaria's farms.

ZAGREB

7 hrs 48 mins

Zagreb is quieter than Croatia's coastal towns, which attract hordes of tourists, but there's plenty to do here for a couple of days. Stroll the pedestrianised Tkalčićeva for decent coffee (coffee fuels most Croatians), take in the masters at the Mimara fine-art museum, and a pre-dinner tipple on Cvetni trg. The Upper Town is the oldest bit of the city and worth a wander round, taking in the cathedral and the Stone Gate before descending back to the present day, via a funicular that takes just over a minute. If you're looking for a party, things start late here and go on and on, and clubs are hidden away in converted factories and even old tennis courts.

TIP

Spend a day at Plitvice Lakes, one of Croatia's most famous national parks and home to 16 cascading blue lakes.

BELGRADE

7 hrs Serbia's capital, Belgrade, is a charming place to break the journey for a couple of days. It sits on the confluence of the Danube and the Sava rivers, where an impressive castle keeps watch. The city fell into so many different empires' hands over the centuries that there's a complete mish-mash of cuisines, architecture and attitudes to entrance you. Serbians play hard, drink hard and eat plenty, so be prepared to have a great time. Head to the riverside for a flotilla of club boats that party till dawn and watch out for Rakia, the local schnapps – it's delicious but lethal.

SOFIA

5 hrs Head into Bulgaria and take in Sofia. While it's not the prettiest city, there is a lot happening here beneath the surface. Start with the red-brick Church of Saint George, built in the fourth-century BC and surrounded by remnants of a Roman street in Serdika, the original settlement.

Sofia is trying to attract more tourists, so there are free walking, street-food and foodie tours across the city. It does have a slightly disjointed feel, with an odd mix of Balkan baroque (the National Theatre) and Communist architecture (the Museum of Socialist Art and the National Palace of Culture), but despite that, there's a real soul to Sofia.

TIP | The train route between Belgrade and Sofia is being updated at the time of writing. An easy alternative is to take the bus.

ISTANBUL

9 hrs* To arrive in Istanbul, you'll need to get off the train at the Turkish border and get a visa, then disembark at Halkalı, just outside Istanbul and get the local train to Sirkeci in the heart of the city. From Topkapı Palace, home to 400 years of sultans, to the enticing Grand Bazar, the ancient streets of Istanbul are laced with exoticism, history and legends. You could spend a week visiting the museums, mosques and ancient monuments, fuelled by the thick-as-mud local coffee. Cross the Golden Horn via Galata Bridge on foot to discover Beyoğlu, the more bohemian side of the city. Use Galata Tower as a landmark and get lost among the tiny cobbled lanes and hipster coffee shops. Head back to the tower at sunset, as it has one of the best views over the mesmerising skyline of Istanbul. *take the overnight train

TIP

Head back via Bucharest and Budapest instead of Sofia and Belgrade.

INDEX

PICTURE CREDITS

P.6 Dom Luis I bridge, Porto, Portugal; Jon Arnold Images Ltd/Alamy Stock Photo **P.8** Ravenna Bridge railway viaduct, Baden-Wurttemberg, Germany; Leonid Andronov/Shutterstock.com **P.9** Parisian Hotel; Huang Zheng/Shutterstock.com **P.10** Gondolas, Venice; Arthur C.C. Hsieh/Shutterstock.com **P.11** Eco- friendly utensils; Almaje/Shutterstock.com **P.14** Bridge of the Canal Saint-Martin, Paris, France; Jerome Labouyrie/Alamy Stock Photo **P.15, left** Gourmet food; Vera Prokhorova/Shutterstock.com **P.15, right** Le Marais, Paris, France; Big Dodzy on Unsplash **P.16, top** Toulouse sausage cassoulet; Simon Dack/Alamy Stock Photo **P.16, bottom** Jardin Japonais, Toulouse; Tibor Bognar/Alamy Stock Photo **P.17, top** Bar Bergara in Gros, San Sebastian; Alex Segre/Alamy Stock Photo **P.17, bottom** Maria Cristina Bridge over the Urumea river, San Sebastian; Leonid Andronov/Shutterstock.com **P.18, left** Bilbao, Spain; Trabantos, Shutterstock.com **P.18, right** Mercado la Ribero, Bilbao; Juan Gomez on Unsplash **P.19, top** Caneles de bordeaux; Piotr Krzeslak/Shutterstock.com **P.19, bottom** Vineyard, Bordeaux; Rudmer Zwerver/Shutterstock.com **P.20** Cheese stall, Naples; DB Pictures/Alamy Stock Photo **P.21, top** Läderach Chocolate Shop, Zurich; Odyssey-Images/Alamy Stock Photo **P.21, bottom** Tropical greenhouses, Zurich Botanical Gardens; Da_Ja_25/Shutterstock.com **P.22, top** Lampredotto sandwich; Atlantide Phototravel/Getty Images **P.22, bottom** Duomo Santa Maria Del Fiore and Bargello, Tuscany; Kavalenkava/Shutterstock.com **P.23, left** Rice croquettes; From my point of view/Shutterstock.com **P.23, right** Dining outside, Rome; Gary Yeowell/Getty Images **P.24, left** Napoli old town at night; Sun_Shine/Shutterstock.com **P.24, right** Seafood at a Naples market; Elxeneize/Alamy Stock Photo **P.25, top** Amalfi coast; Silvia Trigo on Unsplash **P.25, bottom** Medieval market, Bologna; Vivida Photo PC/Shutterstock.com **P.26** Old Nyhavn port, Copenhagen; Nikolay Antonov/Shutterstock.com **P.27, top** Reffen street food market, Copenhagen; Irati Ventoso Cenzano/Shutterstock.com **P.27, bottom** Reffen street food market, Copenhagen; Poludziber/Shutterstock.com **P.28, top** 'Oresundsbron' bridge connecting Sweden with Denmark; Antony McAulay/Shutterstock.com **P.28, bottom left** Malmö Festival; Kimson/Shutterstock.com **P.28, bottom right** Hot chocolate and cinnamon roll, Helsinki; Pojarat Munevanitchakul/Shutterstock.com **P.29, left** Stockholm old town; Mistervlad/Shutterstock.com **P.29, top right** Cyclists in Hammarby Sjöstad, Stockholm; Jeppe Gustafsson/Alamy Stock Photo **P.29, bottom right** Princess cake; Bokehboo Studios/Shutterstock.com **P.30, top** Scandinavian open sandwiches Magdanatka/Shutterstock.com **P.30, bottom** Hjalmaren canal, Arboga; Gigra/Shutterstock.com **P.31, top left** 'Feskekorka' Fish Church, Gothenburg; Nigel Jarvis/Shutterstock.com **P.31, top right** Snack stall, Gothenburg; Mauritius Images GmbH/Alamy Stock Photo **P.31, bottom** Seafood market inside 'Feskekorka' Fish Church, Gothenburg; Mauritius Images GmbH/Alamy Stock Photo **P.34** Galleria Vittorio Emanuele II shopping mall, Milan; Daryan Shamkhali on Unsplash **P.35, top left** Tram, Turin city; Ross-Helen Editorial/Shutterstock.com **P.35, bottom left** Whiskey cocktail, Shyripa Alexandr/Shutterstock.com **P.35, right** Via Garibaldi, main shopping street, Turin; Alessandro Cristiano/Shutterstock.com **P.36, top** Naviglio Grande canal, Milan; Mihai-Bogdan Lazar/Shutterstock.com **P.36, bottom** Galleria Vittorio Emanuele II shopping mall, Milan; Stefano Politi Markovina/Alamy Stock Photo **P.37, top left** Piazza delle Erbe, Verona old town; Jan Wlodarczyk/Alamy Stock Photo **P.37, bottom left** Roman arena, Verona; Nickolay Khoroshkov/Shutterstock.com **P.37, right** 'Juliet's House', Verona; Stefanel/Shutterstock.com **P.38, top** Scala Contarini del Bovolo spiral staircase, Venice; Stephen Fleming/Alamy Stock Photo **P.38, bottom** Traditional canal-side Venetian houses; Nightcap/Shutterstock.com **P.39, top** Portofino town and port; Roman Sigaev/Shutterstock.com **P.39, right** Palazzo Bianco on Via Garibaldi, Genoa; Ian Dagnall/Alamy Stock Photo **P.40** Pilgrimage Church, Neviges; Carlo Polito/Stringer/Getty Images **P.41, top** Noisy-le-Grand, Paris; Ankor Light/Shutterstock.com **P.41, bottom** Noisy-le-Grand Mont d'Est, Paris; Viennaslide/Alamy Stock Photo **P.42** Johannes XXIII Church, Cologne; Joern Sackermann/Alamy Stock Photo **P.43, left** 'Bierpinsel', Berlin; Sueddeutsche Zeitung Photo/Alamy Stock Photo **P.43, top right** Research Institute for Experimental Medicine, Berlin Mo Photography Berlin/Shutterstock.com **P.42, bottom right** König Galerie, Berlin; Schoening/Alamy Stock Photo **P.44** Smolna 8 Tower; Octocore/Shutterstock.com **P.45, top** Bunkier Sztuki Gallery, Krakow; PE Forsberg/Alamy Stock Photo **P.45, bottom** Aerial view of Brno, Moravia; Leonid Andronov/Shutterstock.com **P.46, top** Interior of KonzilsgedaÅNchtniskirche Lainz Speising **P.46, bottom** Kirche Zur Heiligsten Dreifaltigkeit; Hackenberg-Photo-Cologne/Alamy Stock Photo **P.47, left** Town houses, Römerberg; ImageBROKER/Alamy Stock Photo **P.47, right** Deutsche Bahn AG headquarters, Frankfurt Agencja Fotograficzna Caro/Alamy Stock Photo **P.48** East facade and entrance to Valencia Central Market; Peter D Noyce/Alamy Stock Photo **P.49, left** Mercado Central, Valencia **P.49, right** Casa Judia, Castello; Tony Watson/Alamy Stock Photo **P.50, top** La Pedrera, Barcelona; Paul Quayle/Alamy Stock Photo **P.50, bottom** Parc Güell, Barcelona; Vladitto/Shutterstock.com **P.51, bottom** Central Market Hall, Limoges; Liam White/Alamy Stock Photo **P.51, top** Offices of La Depeche du Midi, Toulouse; Mark Dunn/Alamy Stock Photo **P.52, top** Piscine Molitor, Paris; Eric Isselee/Shutterstock.com **P.52, bottom** Villa Cavrois, Lille; BEAUMONT Frédéric/Alamy Stock Photo **P.53, bottom left** Maison Cauchie, Brussels; PjrArt/Alamy Stock Photo **P.53, top right** Hotel Tassel, Brussels; Heritage Image Partnership/Alamy Stock Photo **P.53, bottom right** Museum of Musical Instruments, Brussels; Kiev.Victor/Shutterstock.com **P.56** Glenfinnan Viaduct; Jack Anstey on Unsplash **P.57, left** Dean Village, Edinburgh; Kay Roxby/Alamy Stock Photo **P.57, top right** Arthur's Seat, Holyrood Park, Edinburgh; Udompeter/Shutterstock.com **P.57, bottom right** Victoria Street, Edinburgh; PhotoFires/Shutterstock.com **P.58, top** Forth railway bridge, Edinburgh; Remizov/Shutterstock.com **P.58, bottom** Beach, Fife; Pearl Bucknall/Alamy Stock Photo **P.59, top** Urquart Castle; ReallyEasyStar/Paolo Bolla/Alamy Stock Photo **P.59, bottom** Stream through the Cairngorms, Scottish Highlands, Scotland; Jane Rix/Shutterstock.com **P.60, top** Ben Nevis; Rowan Manning on Unsplash **P.60, bottom** Great Glen Way; Kris Christiaens/Alamy Stock Photo **P.61, top** Loch Lomond; Mairead Warren on Unsplash **P.61, bottom** Mallaig Harbour; Duncan Astbury/Alamy Stock Photo **P.62** Viamala Gorge, River Rhine; Makasana Photo/Shutterstock.com **P.63** Chur, Switzerland; Rudi1976/Alamy Stock Photo **P.64, top** Lake Lugano, Switzerland; MRony/Shutterstock.com **P.64, bottom** Morcote on Lake Lugano, Switzerland; Boris-B/Shutterstock.com **P.65, left** Lake Como; EyeEm/Alamy Stock Photo **P.65, right** The Varenna on Lake Como; Nattee Chalermtiragool/Alamy Stock Photo **P.66, top** Footpath towards Monte Resegone; Michele D'Amico supersky77/Getty Images **P.66, bottom** Vineyards, Costiera dei Cech, Valtellina; Roberto Moiola/Sysaworld/Getty Images **P.67** Bernina Express, Lombardy; Andreas Stutz on Unsplash **P.68** Geroldsau Waterfall, Black Forest; diiidiii205/Shutterstock.com **P.69, top** Volksgarten Park, Cologne; Chris Hoppe on Unsplash **P.69, bottom** Cologne Cathedral with Hohenzollern Bridge; Lucas Carl on Unsplash **P.70, top** Cable cars, Koblenz; Julia Solonina on Unsplash **P.70, bottom** Eltz Castle between

terstock.com **P.146** Torimbia beach, Asturias; David Acosta Allely/Alamy Stock Photo **P.147, top** La Salvé beach, Laredo; Derek Evans/Alamy Stock Photo **P.147, bottom** Laredo town; Greens and Blues/Shutterstock.com **P.148, left** Playa de Berria, Cantabria Ian Thraves/Alamy Stock Photo **P.148, top right** Marismas de Santona Natural Park, Santoña Mikel Bilbao/VWPics/Alamy Stock Photo **P.148, bottom right** Faro del Caballo on Mount Buciero, Santoña; A.B.G./Shutterstock.com **P.149** Aerial view of Santander; Saiko3p/Shutterstock.com **P.150, top left** Santillana del Mar, Cantabria; David Bagnall/Alamy Stock Photo **P.150, bottom left** Altamira cave, Santillana del Mar, Cantabria Jesus De Fuensanta/Shutterstock.com **P.150, right** Santa Justa cave chapel, Ubiarco, Cantabria Agefotostock/Alamy Stock Photo **P.151** Torimbia beach, Asturias; David Acosta Allely/Alamy Stock Photo **P.152, top** Naranjo de Bulnes (known as Picu Urriellu), Asturias; Anton Petrus/Shutterstock.com **P.152, bottom** Oviedo Cathedral, LucVi/Shutterstock.com **P.153, left** Cimadevilla M Ramirez/Alamy Stock Photo **P.153, right** Camp Valdes Roman baths, Gijon; Agefotostock/Alamy Stock Photo **P.154** Giant's Causeway; Ester Lo Feudo/Shutterstock.com **P.155, top** The Peace Bridge, Londonderry/ Derry; Dennis Frates/Alamy Stock Photo **P.155, bottom** Mussenden Temple, Benone Strand, Catlerock; Clearview/Alamy Stock Photo **P.156, top** Portstewart bech, County Antrim; UAV 4/Shutterstock.com **P.156, bottom** Carrick-a-Rede Rope Bridge; MNStudio/Shutterstock.com **P.157, top** Belfast Botanic Gardens, Queen's Quarter, Belfast; Oxford Picture Library/Alamy Stock Photo **P.157, bottom** The 'Big Fish' sculpture by John Kindness, Lagan Weir, Belfast; Lowefoto/alamy Stock Photo **P.158, top** Ha'penny Bridge, Dublin; Madrugada Verde/Shutterstock.com **P.158, bottom** Sorrento Point and Dalkey Island; Robert Kelly/Alamy Stock Photo **P.159, left** The Powerscourt Waterfall, Powerscourt Estate House and Gardens, Enniskerry; Tracey Whitefoot/Alamy Stock Photo **P.159, right** Cliff walk from Bray to Greystones Grethe Ulgjell/Alamy Stock Photo **P.162, left** The Trenino Verde in Gairo station, Sardinia Radek Vicar/Shutterstock.com **P.163, left** Giants Tomb of Coddu Vecchiu, Nuragic necropolis, Arzachena, Sardinia ArtMediaFactory/Shutterstock.com **P.163, right** Punta dei Capriccioli Beach, Sardinia Jan Wlodarczyk/Alamy Stock Photo **P.164, top** Bosa old town, Sardinia; Jan Wlodarczyk/Alamy Stock Photo **P.164, bottom** Macomer, Italy; Salvatore Cherchi/EyeEm/Getty Images **P.165, left** Aymerich Laconi waterfall; Fabiano Goreme Caddeo/shutterstock.com **P.165, right** Nuraghe Orolo near Macomer, Sardinia; Rainer Hackenberg/Getty Images **P.166, top** Mountain biking, Monte Corrasi, Sardinia; Roberto Nencini/Alamy Stock Photo **P.166, bottom** San Valentino Waterfall A. Enrico/Shutterstock.com **P.167, top** Ruins of the abandoned ghost town Gairo Vecchio, Sardinia; Vanna Moro/Shutterstock.com **P.167, middle** Tomba dei Giganti, Bosco

di Selene; Ivana Barrili/ Shutterstock.com **P.167, bottom** Mountain village of Tortoli Agencja Fotograficzna Caro/Alamy Stock Photo **P.168** Medieval street in old Riga, Latvia; Sergei25/Shutterstock.com **P.169, top** Kaunas old town, Lithuania; Finn Stock/Shutterstock.com **P.169, bottom** Aerial view of Kaunus, Lithuania; Madrugada Verde **P.170, top** Mural, Vilnius; Peter Ptschelinzew/Alamy Stock Photo **P.170, bottom** Aerial view of Panev žys; Martynas Charevicius/Shutterstock.com **P.171** House of the Blackheads, Riga, Latvia; S-F/Shutterstock.com **P.172** Gauja National Park; Viesturs Jugs/Shutterstock.com **P.173, top** Ski jump, Tehvandi, Estonia; Yllar Hendla/Alamy Stock Photo **P.173, bottom** Alexander Nevsky Cathedral, Tallinn Old Town, Estonia; TTstudio/Shutterstock.com **P.174** Northern lights over Jokkmokk and Lake Talvatis, Swedish Lapland Sabine Hortebusch/Alamy Stock Photo **P.175, top** Sami Reindeer Martens Tom **P.175, bottom** Castle, Gällivare; Northsweden/Shutterstock.com **P.176, top left** Jokkmokk, Swedish Lapland; Scandphoto/Shutterstock.com **P.176, bottom left** Red fox, Jokkmokk, Swedish Lapland; Mats Lindberg/Alamy Stock Photo **P.176, right** Dog sledge crossing Lake Talvatis, Jokkmokk, Swedish Lapland; Dave Stevenson/Alamy Stock Photo **P.177** Vildmarksvägen wilderness trail, Lapland; Karin Jaehne/Shutterstock.com **P.178, top left** Kayaking at Wild Jamtland nature reserve, Sweden; Sander van der Werf/Shutterstock.com **P.178, bottom left** Lake, Östersund; Stefan Johansson980/Shutterstock.com **P.178, right** Mountain railroad at the ski resort in Åre, Sweden; Tommy Alven/Shutterstock.com **P.179** The Dala Horse, Mora, Sweden, Michael715/Shutterstock.com **P.182** Roman baths, Bath; Claudio Divizia/Shutterstock.com **P.183, top** Platform 9 3/4 at Kings Cross Station, London; Hethers/Shutterstock.com **P.183, bottom** Windsor Castle, Berkshire; Moomusician/Shutterstock.com **P.184** Bath, Somerset Valdis Skudre/Shutterstock.com **P.185, top** Brunel's *SS Great Britain*, Bristol waterfront; Sion Hannuna/Shutterstock.com **P.185, bottom** Cyclists on Taff Trail, River Taff, Cardiff Graham Bell/Alamy Stock Photo **P.186** Disneyland, Paris Kevin Williams/Alamy Stock Photo **P.187** Mad Hatter's tea cup ride at Disneyland, Paris; SJH Photography/Alamy Stock Photo **P.188, top** Europa Park; Eva Bocek/ Shutterstock.com **P.188, bottom** Poseidon water roller coaster in the Greece-themed area of Europa Park Preisler/Shutterstock.com **P.189** Toverland, Netherlands Attraction Images/Shutterstock.com **P.190, top** Animated tree in Efteling theme park, Kaatsheuvel, Netherlands; Laurens Smak/Alamy Stock Photo **P.190, bottom** Gnome village in Efteling theme park, Kaatsheuvel, Netherlands; Julia700702/Shutterstock.com **P.191, top** Water slides at Duinrell theme park, Wassenaar, Netherlands; Justin Long/Alamy Stock Photo **P.191, bottom** Walibi theme park, Brussels; Claire Slingerland/Alamy Stock Photo **P.192** Mount Pilatus cable car above Lucerne, Switzerland; JB-2078/Alamy Stock Photo **P.193** Cruise vessel on Riv-

er Limmat, Zurich; Aldorado/Alamy Stock Photo **P.194, top** Summer toboggan run, Lucerne; Vincenzo Cagnuzzo/Alamy Stock Photo **P.194, bottom** Cable car traveling towards Pilatus Kulm, Lucerne; Arvid Norberg/Alamy Stock Photo **P.195** Grindelwald village, Berne, Switzerland; 145Patma/Shutterstock.com **P.196, top** Bear park, Bern Prisma by Dukas Presseagentur GmbH/Alamy Stock Photo **P.196, bottom** 'Chocolate Express' train at Montreux station; Serjio74/Shutterstock.com **P.197** Yvonand beach, Lake Neuchatel, Switzerland; Bogdan Lazar/Alamy Stock Photo **P.200** Naeroyfjord, Norway; Maria Uspenskaya/Shutterstock.com **P.201, top** Norsk Folkemuseum, Oslo; Hemis/Alamy Stock Photo **P.201, bottom** Sculpture by Gustav Vigeland, Vigeland Park, Oslo; Yelo Jura/Shutterstock.com **P.202, top** Flam railway; Alex Jackson/Shutterstock.com **P.202, bottom** Kayaking in the Nærøyfjord, Norway Gaute Ulltang/Shutterstock.com **P.203, top** Kjosfossen waterfall between Flam and Myrdal INTREEGUE Photography/Shutterstock.com **P.203, bottom** Cycling down to Flam on the Sognefjord, Myrdal; Atlantide Phototravel/Getty Images **P.204, top** Bryggen-Hanseatic wharf, Bergen, Norway; Olena Tur/Shutterstock.com **P.204, bottom left** Waterfall, Bergen Michael Thaler/Alamy Stock Photo **P.204, bottom right** Whitewater rafting, West Coast rivers, Norway Steve Bly/Shutterstock.com **P.205** Geilo, Norway Simen Brurberg/500px/Getty Images **P.206** Dragon Bridge, Ljubljana, Slovenia Matej Kastelic/Shutterstock.com **P.207, top** Canals and restaurants, Trieste Leoks/Shutterstock.com **P.207, bottom** Tivoli Park, Ljubljana, Slovenia MPMP/Shutterstock.com **P.208, top** Annual diving competition on River Soca, Kanal, Slovenia; Luka Dakskobler/Xinhua/Alamy Live News **P.208, bottom** Steam Train on Solkan Bridge, Primorska, Slovenia; Pavliha/Getty Images **P.209, top** Solkan Kayak Center, Nova Gorica, Slovenia; sn0wball1/Shutterstock.com **P.209, bottom** Goriška brda vineyard region, western Slovenia; Nejc Trpin/Alamy Stock Photo **P.210** Grotta Gigante cave network, Trieste Sergei Bogomyakov/Alamy Stock Photo **P.211, top** Catholic Cathedral, Zagreb; Ilija Ascic/Shutterstock.com **P.211, bottom** Cycling by river, Zagreb; Nino Marcutti/Alamy Stock Photo **P.212** Istanbul skyline Travel Turkey/Shutterstock.com **P.213, top** Little Venice, Regent's Canal, London; I Wei Huang / Shutterstock.com **P.213, bottom** Jardin des Tuileries, Paris Jean Luclchard/Shutterstock.com **P.214, bottom left** Breakfast coffee and pastry Tastytim/Shutterstock.com **P.214, top right** Müellersches Volksbad swimming pool, Munich FooT Too/Shutterstock.com **P.214, bottom right** Street food, Marienplatz, Munich Franz12/Shutterstock.com **P.215** Upper town walkway, Zagreb xbrchx/Shutterstock.com **P.216, top** Fortress archway, River Danube, Belgrade PhotoEdit/Alamy Stock Photo **P.216, bottom** National Place of Culture, Sofia Ana Flašker/Alamy Stock Photo **P.217** Grand Bazaar, Istanbul; Tekkol/Shutterstock.com